THE FULL
SCOOP ON BS

PETER DUNCAN

Order this book online at www.trafford.com
or email orders@trafford.com

Most Trafford titles are also available at major online book retailers.

Printed in the United States of America.

ISBN: 978-1-4907-2776-9 (sc)
ISBN: 978-1-4907-2775-2 (e)

Trafford rev. 04/17/2014

Trafford
PUBLISHING   www.trafford.com
North America & international
toll-free: 1 888 232 4444 (USA & Canada)
fax: 812 355 4082

Dedicated to my late father, Peter Scheffel, about whom it was said, "He has more stories than The Bible".

TABLE OF CONTENTS

PREFACE

Reading this book will be the most life-changing experience of your year. You may have just formed an opinion as to whether or not my opening sentence is BS. If you have, you may be right, wrong, or a bit of each. The problem is, you may not *know*, not yet anyway. First and perhaps most importantly, you may not know whether or not my statement is BS because you may not know what BS *is*? A lot of people don't. This is well illustrated by a recent conversation I had with a friend I'll refer to as Chas, chiefly because his name is Chas.

About a month before I started writing this book, I went to a busy mall to use an automated bank machine. I drove my car into a parking space and walked about 30 yards to the mall, on the way running into Chas. I have issues with lazy people so when I saw a guy sitting in the driver's seat of a car parked illegally in a fire route immediately outside the mall entrance, and jamming up the area for people trying to drive to nearby parking spaces, I walked up to the driver's window for a few words.

"I parked over there in a parking spot." I said, making sure to keep a polite tone and smile, "You know why?"

"No?" the unsuspecting driver said in a confused tone.

"Because *I* don't think I'm *special* and I'm not *lazy*." Maintaining my smile, I then asked, "Get what I mean?"

Were I alone, you can imagine what the guy may have told me to do. However, as I spoke with the driver, Chas was working and walked up in the police uniform he wears for what he and his colleagues call *the job.* So the driver said what he wanted *Chas* to hear: "I'm just waiting for my wife. She's just in the drug store."

Perhaps his wife was physically disabled, which would have made me feel awful, "Geez, I'm sorry. Is she disabled?"

More confusion followed. "Huh? No?" Then the driver, for the first time in our short exchange, thought and soon after drove to a parking spot. After I went into the mall, used the ATM and came out, the guy was standing outside the drug store waiting for his wife. He seemed in no mortal danger or discomfort I could see. He just sported an awkward grin.

With fresh cash in hand, I lined up in a coffee shop within the mall to buy Chas a coffee; cops don't get freebies nearly much as some might believe. Chatting with him about the exchange, from which he got quite a chuckle, I mentioned how easy it is to tell someone is BSing when they throw out a clear indicator of that. In the driver's case, it was "I was just . . ." Chas is an experienced and committed cop, which means he is highly skilled at catching BS. So, I was surprised when he started talking about how cues for lies aren't always correct. I agree and a growing body of research does too, but I wasn't talking about *lies.* I was talking about BS, a whole other beast altogether.

This isn't to slam Chas. He and most of his colleagues are supposed to be very good at detecting BS *and* lies, and no doubt a lot of them are. Since Chas didn't know the difference between BS and lies, though, and he sees a lot of both every work day, I figured a lot of other people probably don't either. Soon after, my work here began.

When people make statements or claims, tell stories or posit arguments, those on the receiving end do not necessarily know if what they are told is true and accurate. A lot of other people don't care if it's true so long as it's something they *want* to hear. Such is the nature of BS. It is nothing new. It has been around since before any of us *were* us. It hasn't changed in form since before there was a name for it. Easily accessible air travel makes many diseases far more contagious and by extension quite dangerous. In the same way, easily accessible media make BS far wider-spread and sometimes also quite dangerous.

On the brighter side of BS, and there is one, it's funny how many people get sucked into loops of self-perpetuating poop and how easy those piles are to avoid. Some people with little to no education have a skilled nose for recognizing BS. Others with several academic letters after their names eat up and regurgitate the stuff with reckless abandon. There is a very simple reason for this.

Conventional education has very little to do with BS recognition. It should and it can, but it often doesn't. BS busting skills are largely developed in functional, free thinking families, classrooms, and friendships during casual conversation. If you didn't grow up in a functional family, don't worry about it because I didn't either. In my late 20s and quite by accident, I stumbled over the keys to recognizing BS, stopping it in its tracks, and help other people recognize it too.

While researching at-risk youth issues, I recognized the single most influential factor in dysfunctional living whether addictions, teen parenting, gang life, terrorism, preventable health problems, bad driving, or most social ills. Given the topic of this book, you can probably guess what that factor is. Just like driving a car well, the requisite skills for dealing with BS are easily accessible, they can be simply taught, and they can quickly become subconscious, automatic, and instilled for life. Simple, huh? Not quite.

While many people drive, not all of us drive *well*. Remarkably few bad drivers believe *they* do that poorly. Some of the worst offenders truly believe they drive well. Many aspects of thinking work the same way.

I don't want to abolish BS, see new laws limiting it, or any steps so drastic. BS is often the basis for comedy and sometimes vital for graciousness, politeness, or to avoid deep hurt. Most husbands don't tell their wives they look "a bit chunky" even if they think their wives do. Most dads don't tell a four-year-old daughter she sucks at ballet even if she does a face plant at dance class. Most wives don't tell their husbands they are idiots even when they think they are, at least at that moment. Okay, I may be pushing it with the last one. Nevertheless, a world devoid of BS would be rude, humourless, potentially hostile, and less passionate.

Trying to eradicate BS would be like kicking in your family doctor's office door for dealing drugs, or accusing your son's pee wee soccer coach of fraud for telling kids they're doing well even when they aren't. Moderation, control, and purpose are the keys to safe handling of this otherwise smelly substance.

Whether or not this book changes your life will depend on how much BS you dish out, how much you consume, if you understand what BS is, and if you know the difference between a pinch and a truckload of the stuff. For an awful long time I couldn't tell the difference, although you may be a lot smarter than me. I mean that. Really. No BS.

INTRODUCTION

When discussing most topics, in books or conversations or classrooms, it is important to make sure everyone knows what you are talking about, to define what the topic actually is. It is also important *you* know what you are talking about. When the topic is a single word or term, it makes particular sense to start with a definition. Be that as it may, BS and the well known term that abbreviation conveys is a topic which requires a few ground rules in order to avoid a detailed look *at* BS being smothered *by* it.

In 1972, famed American comic George Carlin first performed his famous monologue entitled "The Seven Words You Can Never Say on Television". Those words were considered highly inappropriate in broadcast media, books, and conversation within polite society, yet each was known then and is commonly known to most people today, including those who never *say* them. They are identifiable for most people when abbreviated as S, P, F, C, MF, CS and T. I'm sure everyone knows what word "BS" refers to whether they say that word or not.

I don't use the abbreviation *BS* here for brevity or to be polite. I simply want to remove one excuse some people might cite for not discussing what is normally known by the full word, that it is rude to use profanity. I want to

1

make discussion of BS acceptable on mainstream media, and in conversation within classrooms, among families, workplaces, and in polite society.

Written English has common abbreviations such as *Inc.* for Incorporated and *Ltd.* for Limited. In English, readers can pronounce the abbreviation or the word for which it stands. For instance, when readers see "Apple Inc." on a page, they can internally hear Apple *Ink* or Apple *Incorporated*, whichever they prefer. By contrast, written Spanish uses the written form *Ud.* to represent a word that is pronounced as *oosted* (meaning *you*) in all instances. Just as readers of Spanish always think and internally hear *oosted* when they read *Ud.*, I think it is important that you internally hear the full word when you read *BS* in these pages. Although not always appropriate, profanity can be helpful when used sparingly to emphasize something dirty, repugnant, or extreme in one way or another. Two letters simply do not capture the essence of how repugnant and sometimes extreme BS can be. Incidentally, I use "BS" in brackets to avoid using the actual word when referring to other people's work that has the full word within it.

So let's make a deal right here: I will type the two letters and you will *hear* the word those letters represent. In that way, neither you nor I will offend polite society, which can't control what we think or hear inside our heads. While often gracious and useful, most polite societies of the past were remarkably impolite with some of their own people. Some in ancient times practiced human sacrifice. Others used religious persecution, torture, and death by means ranging from burning to hanging to beheading. Polite society in the American South before the American Civil War condoned slavery of people ethnically descended from Africa. Hence, to a certain extent at least, the concept of polite society is itself BS.

With the exception of MF and CS, the seven dirty words are merely profane versions of acceptable words, if not ones discussed in today's polite societies. There are, and always have been, other words used to describe that which is best known today as BS. They used to include *humbug* and *hokum*. They currently include *rubbish, balderdash, baloney* and a host of others. Once in a while, though, people speaking in one language come up with a word so fitting to what it describes that it spreads to other languages too.

When a *tsunami* in the Indian Ocean wiped out hundreds of thousands of people, no one worried about it being a Japanese word. When someone sticks a pin in a doll to cause pain to the person depicted by that doll, it is referred to by the Dehomy (West-African dialect) word *voodoo* even if it happens in the Dominican Republic or New York. When American parents send their children to school before the first grade, those children attend *kindergarten* even if they never learn German, from which the word originated. BS describes a particular thing in a way that evokes a response or recognition, that what is described may not be the worst thing in the world but stinks a bit nonetheless. The term is recognized in several other languages as well.

So, what *is* BS? Most people who write will build on earlier works from other people. In defining BS, I was greatly assisted by the work of Harry G. Frankfurt. People with significant academic credentials are sometimes viewed as pompous or pretentious by those without them. Since pomposity and pretentiousness enable BS, less-educated folks like me are wise to beware of such traits. Yet Harry Frankfurt, Professor Emeritus of Philosophy at Princeton University, appears decidedly without either trait, not just because he went by the informal *Harry*. He examined fundamental issues of morality in ways that laymen such as I could understand, consider, discuss, and integrate into our own thoughts. One of Professor Frankfurt's best known essays was his bestselling *On (BS)*, in which he shed considerable light onto defining BS. That isn't as easy as some might otherwise believe. Almost no one would suggest it is a statement of truth yet many believe it is a lie. It is neither. By its very nature, BS lays somewhere between the truth and lies. Clear as mud, right?

In the simplest of terms, which do little justice to Frankfurt's essay, BS is something that is not true but is short of a lie. If something is untrue, is it not by default a lie? Not necessarily. Frankfurt examined the difference between liars and (BSers):

> Telling a lie is an act of sharp focus. It is designed to insert a particular falsehood at a specific point in a set or system of beliefs, in order to avoid the consequences of having that point occupied by the truth. This requires a degree of craftsmanship, in which the teller of the lie submits to objective constraints imposed by what he takes to be the truth. The liar is inescapably concerned with truth-values. In order to invent a lie at all, he must think he knows what is true. And in order to invent an effective lie, he must design his falsehood under the guidance of the truth.

> One the other hand, a person who undertakes to (BS) his way through has much more freedom. His focus is panoramic rather than particular. He does not limit himself to inserting a certain falsehood at a specific point, and thus he is not constrained by the truths surrounding that point or intersecting it. He is prepared to fake context as well, so far as need requires.

What is true and accurate is not merely an academic concern. These are the concerns of most *reasonable* people. Who wants to be lied to? Who wants to be sold a bill of goods or a load of ideas based on lies? What Frankfurt points out, though, is that someone can tell you something that is *not* a lie but that still falls well short of the truth.

In our day-to-day existence, worrying about whether or not someone lies or merely tells BS might be considered an *academic exercise*, a term that some take to mean *pointless.* Yet as Frankfurt's next excerpt made clear, that is not the case at all:

> It is impossible for someone to lie unless he thinks he knows the truth. Producing (BS) requires no such conviction. A person who lies is thereby responding to the truth, and he is to that extent respectful of it. When an honest man speaks, he says only what he believes to be true; and for the liar, it is correspondingly indispensable that he consider his statements to be false. For the (BSer), however, all bets are off: he is neither on the side of the true nor on the side of the false. His eye is not on the facts at all, as the eyes of the honest man and the liar are, except insofar as they may be pertinent to his interest in getting away with what he says. He does not care whether the things he says describe reality correctly. He picks them out, or makes them up, to suit is purpose.

Some people believe they can spot liars, cheats, and the like. Even if some people *can* spot liars, and considerable research suggests otherwise, that gift may be useless with BSers, some who *believe* what they say, and some who have no regard for what the truth is. Arguably, a polygraph may be of little use since those machines measure symptoms of physiological stress widely believed to be exhibited during the telling of a lie. When there is no care for what the truth is, or no knowledge of that, there is far less likelihood of stress being demonstrated by the BSing subject. Fortunately, we don't need special gifts or equipment to pick off many liars *or* BSers. With a fairly modest introduction to a few skills, and with a bit of practice, any of us can be as effective at picking off BSers as today's children are at picking off monsters in video games.

In my opinion, BS-busting is as important for average laypeople as it is for academics and researchers. Most people form beliefs and opinions, make decisions, and act on those decisions, all based on what information we get from other people. They include conversations at work, on the bus, in casual meetings, even in local taverns or pubs. They include various media such as television reports, talk radio, printed media and, of course, the Internet.

Although part of the word is similar, there's a big difference between BS and mere *bull*. As Frankfurt explained:

> What tends to go on in a bull session is that the participants try out various thoughts and attitudes in order to see how it feels to hear them selves saying such things and in order to discover how others respond, without it being assumed that they are committed to what they say. It is understood by everyone in a bull session that the statements people make do not necessarily reveal what they really believe or how they really feel.

Frankfurt went on to clarify,

> Each of the contributors to a bull session relies, in other words, upon a general recognition that what he expresses or says is not to be understood as being what he means wholeheartedly or believes unequivocally to be true.

Thus, if a friend in the gym slapped me on the chest and struck a fighting stance, I wouldn't think he was attacking me. If a woman said she would quit if that bastard Johnson became the boss, no one would expect her to pack up her desk if Johnson actually did. Even if someone refers to it as a BS session or BSing around, the kind of bull tossed about is implicitly understood to be something far less than true without the suggestion it is true. That is why bull is so harmless and why it differs considerably from BS.

Arguably, some BS borders on mere bull, particularly when used in comedy or fiction. When a comedian tells the crowd her husband is so fat that Greenpeace ships escort him when he swims, everyone realizes the comic's husband could just as easily be a male model for all they know. Some shows, such as the Colbert Report, are complete spoofs of the very kind of person Stephen Colbert publicly presents himself as. Again, the satire is so extreme, everyone gets that it is bull.

When it comes to actual BS, it is handy to develop the ability to recognize it when you see it, hear it, or smell it. Tune into a daytime talk show of the tell-all variety, if only for a minute so your brain doesn't seize up. The likes of Jerry Springer and Mauri Povich come to mind but there are many others. Focus on any person on the program, whether on stage or in the peanut gallery. Whichever freak you see, that person can send all sorts of feces your way. Blogs and websites are so easy to set up that virtually anyone with fingers can put whatever he wants onto the web. After that, his beliefs and opinions are every bit as accessible as Professor Frankfurt's most researched work. How's *that* for freedom of speech?

Naturally, a full set of teeth doesn't prevent one from shovelling truckloads of BS. Someone who precedes his statement with, 'I read on the net that . . ." may be no better informed than the village idiot. Moreover, some *poo tossers* have several academic credentials, loyal audiences, or both.

Caution is required when considering what to swallow or not, yet a landscape littered with steaming heaps is not any more hazardous today than in decades past. The speed and volume of media throw forth all manner of stink, but true and accurate information arrive by those same means. The poop/truth ratio may have remained steady in that period. No reliable source indicates otherwise. Still, with more information streaming at us every day from a variety of sources, there is always the danger of that ratio shifting. Accuracy requires homework, fact checking, and consideration of what you are putting out there. This isn't Olympic weight lifting yet it is more work than average BSers puts into what they post, write, say, or casually utter. Furthermore, an increasing number of people grow addicted to all things fast, quick and easy. *Short is sweet*, the belief goes. Short, quick information often has the same intellectual value as sugar coated doughnuts have dietary value.

Not all people have the same metabolism or intellectual potential. Yet genetics need not play as much of a determining role as some people allow it to. Many people with hereditary weight issues control those with different choices, after a problem emerges or even before. Most people who believe themselves less intellectually equipped than others can similarly surpass the low expectations set for them, or by them. Healthy eating results from choosing what to and what not to (literally) swallow. BS filtering occurs after information is taken in but well before it is metaphorically swallowed.

I don't suggest any form of censorship, whether for BS or other hazards. Who would decide on what to be censored? Besides, that has been tried many times in many places to little useful effect. Many immigrant groups and some of our own ancestors have been there, done that.

What seems more effective to my limited intellect is an audience better prepared to filter the foulest smelling piles. BS is dropped upon most paths we stroll along but that doesn't oblige us to step in every pile the way someone with Obsessive Compulsive Disorder might step on every sidewalk crack. A side step now and again will usually suffice.

How do you become a BS buster, or get better at that if you have already taken up the hobby? Well, the skills required for better living are *simple* to achieve although not *easy*, despite many people inferring the two are synonymous. BS busting takes a little work, although only in an intellectual sense. Once begun, most people want to continue BS busting. Furthermore, that which initially takes a lot of effort becomes easier with practice, just as walking, talking, bathing, and eating solid food become almost automatic with practice.

In his essay, "How to Detect Propaganda", Clyde Miller provided readers with ways to do just that, *propaganda* often being BS of the highest order. He spoke directly to the effort and rewards for that:

> Why are we fooled by these devices? Because they appeal to our emotions rather than to our reason. They make us believe and do something we would not believe or do if we thought about it calmly, dispassionately. In examining these

devices, note that *they work most effectively at those times when we are too lazy to think for ourselves,* also, they tie into emotions which sway us to be "for" or "against" nations, races, religions, ideals, economic and political policies and practices, and so on through automobiles, cigarettes, radios, toothpastes, presidents, and wars. With our emotions stirred, it may be fun to be fooled by these devices, but *it is more fun and infinitely more to our own interests* to know how they work (italics added).

As with many skills we use from time to time, we can choose when to commence BS busting. These skills don't get in the way of a good bull session, a funny joke, watching a comedy show, or any scenario wherein a sprinkle of BS is called for. There are times, though, when BS busting is precisely what makes the difference between success and failure, between functionality and disaster. What do terrorists and gang bangers have in common? How about teenaged parents and drug addicts? How about some voters, and no matter who they vote for? Given the topic, you can guess what but you may not yet grasp how or why that is the case. Of course, you may believe I'm BSing. There's only one way to find out.

LANGUAGE

In an earlier book, I addressed what I believe are the keys to functional living, what I called the *Core Skills*. People who live functionally most often have those skills to varying degrees. The more of these skills individual people have and the better they are at them, the more functional and successful those folks seem to be. Seems fairly simple, right? That depends on *language*.

As we will see, all kinds of BS can get in the way of functionality and success. This suggests a link between these core skills and keeping the bottoms of your shoes clean. Since functionality and clean shoe bottoms may be linked, and the keys to functionality are simple, it would seem fairly simple to avoid BS, no? That too depends on language.

Language provides more protection against dirty shoes than many people appreciate. It is the difference between a wise man and a wise ass. Stated in accurate language, what the core skills are and how they can help people are both very simple. The trouble is that some people don't know what *simple* really means.

Being a light infantryman in the First World War was remarkably simple. One simply did what he was told, when he was told, exactly how he was told. If he was ordered to go *over the top,* it was remarkably simple. It didn't matter how many machine guns or mortars were pointed his way once he left the relative protection of his trench to charge across open fields toward the bad guys firing from the cover of their trenches. The task was frightening, difficult, often deadly, yet that in no way detracted from the simplicity of it. Here's what that horror show definitely wasn't: *easy.* That's a whole other matter entirely. *Easy* is to *simple* as *baby making* is to *child rearing.*

I suggest the reason why so many people are missing core skills is because those require knowledge *and* work to acquire. Many dysfunctional people are far from lazy, but a skill is difficult to acquire without the required knowledge *and* practice, often lots of the latter. Am I suggesting that *no* dysfunctional people are lazy? Don't be a wise ass. Some dysfunctional people lack the knowledge. Some lack the willingness to turn that knowledge into practiced skills. Some lack both.

Each core skill is used separately in some instances and in combination with others in other instances. These are the Core Skills I examined in an earlier work:

Basic Life Skills—Properly sleeping, eating, personal hygiene; dressing properly, physical fitness, and other necessary skills for every-day life.

Communication—The written and spoken word, non-verbal communication such as personal actions and art forms. Receiving information and effectively expressing needs, opinions, and questions.

Critical Thinking—Effectively arguing ideas with someone else or oneself (the latter being decision making). This is vital to finding the truth in any statement or belief. It allows effective interaction between people with differing views.

Lateral Processes—Thinking creatively, and applying experience or lessons from one area to others. These processes allow one to learn from other's mistakes instead of making them all oneself, and they allow thinking in creative ways to solve problems.

Using Rules—Doing the right thing because it helps, not just because the rules say to. Working within a group instead of against it. Understanding what rules are, why they exist, and how they can be changed if they are wrong. When someone breaks a rule, either they are wrong or the rule is. This skill enables people to correct whichever is wrong.

When it comes to BS busting, Communication and Critical Thinking are vital. The latter skill allows you (meaning anyone) to think logically, express yourself the same way, detect a lack of logic in other people's messages, make reasonable decisions about those messages, and figure out what is true. Without communication skills, specifically *language*, critical thinking does not occur.

In some cases, poor language skills are the cause of BS. Had you been a First World War infantryman in the trenches, you might have been told by your Sergeant at some point, "Our job tonight is bloody simple, Lads. Just charge the Huns' trenches and drive them off."

Without a clear understanding of language, in this case the meaning of *simple,* you might have yelled back, "This isn't simple! It's crazy and I'm not going!" A patient man in a different place and time might have pointed out your misunderstanding of the word. Had this scenario been real for you, the Sergeant would have probably shot you on the spot for cowardice before other guys started protesting. Simple!

Critical thinking, known by terms such as *critical reasoning, deductive reasoning, applied logic* and others, is growing in popularity, unfortunately only in one sense. It is referred to increasingly by well-meaning people who speak of its importance in modern society. Sadly, far more people talk about it than actually understand it, use it, or teach it.

Critical thinking is remarkably simple too, in the same way that advanced mathematics is. The principles and formulas of each field apply without exception. Once someone knows those principles and formulas, it is very simple to figure problems out, whether those are complex math problems or if someone's words are accurate and true. In the next chapter, I address the most important skill for effective BS busting, critical thinking, which I refer to in this book as *reasoning*. Inasmuch as that skill starts with accurate use of language, to discuss reasoning now would be the same as addressing advanced mathematics before ensuring you know what algebraic symbols are and what they mean.

Obviously, you have language skills or you would be unable to read this. That saves us both a lot of work. Without knowing you, it is quite possible your language skills are considerably stronger than mine. You may also speak two languages or perhaps several. It is also possible your language skills are weaker than mine, if only slightly weaker and only in *this* language.

Some time ago I heard a hurried mother of two say, "I'm losing my scruples." She probably heard other people say they were losing their *marbles*, misheard the last word in that common expression of feeling overwhelmed, and then substituted it with the similar sounding *scruples*. This mother had her kids with her, so I'm sure she wasn't announcing that she was losing her conscience, principles, ethics, or sense of right and wrong, words you may know are synonymous with *scruples*.

Who am I to judge when it comes to errors in language? I have a busy brain so my mother used to tell me I looked *pensive* and should relax. I assumed *relaxed* was the opposite of *pensive* (*pensive* and *tense* even sounded similar to me, so I thought it meant tense or aggravated). *Pensive* means *thoughtful*, so my mother meant I should *mentally* relax. "I'm perfectly relaxed." I said defensively to my spouse years later when she said I looked pensive. "Why do you think I'm pissed off?" She didn't know what the heck I was talking about. As it turned out, I didn't either.

A few small language glitches don't make someone incapable of reasoning yet understanding the meaning of what is argued is vital. Many large and small disagreements stem from someone misunderstanding one or two key words, so one of the first steps in reasoning is to accurately understand what someone means by what he says. That way, you can be for or against what someone *actually* means instead of what you *believe* that person means.

Does responsibility for understanding always fall on the listener or reader? It may seem that way, especially when you're part of a large audience or away from the source. How can you clarify, for instance, what someone says on CNN? Many people who are heard or read by others make all sorts of mistakes. You are almost sure to hear such errors during the course of a lengthy news cast. In reasoning, you are not responsible for what someone else says. Still, you can clarify what a person means with some degree of accuracy, or you can reason out how much weight to give a source based on how well he expresses himself or herself. For example, when I refer to a hypothetical person as *he*, some people may believe I am sexist or that I mean only men can make mistakes. If you read varied sources regularly, you will know how often the mention of the male gender refers to both or either.

It is the same in Spanish and many other languages. For instance, *padre* means *father* in Spanish whereas *padres* means *parents*.

If you are not yet well read, and even if this is the first book you have committed to read, you still have options. You can ask someone else who reads regularly, Google the issue, or contact a human-rights organization if you're concerned I might have a gender bias. With these approaches and others, you can avoid getting angry over nothing more sinister than common English usage.

Sadly, misunderstandings often turn into disagreements, after which come mistaken beliefs and opinions. Consider the court system. When a man (or woman!) is found *not guilty* in a legal trial, many people assume the person was proven innocent when that is rarely true.

There exists within many courts systems, the British, American, Australian, and Canadian to name just four, a presumption of innocence. An accused person, or his lawyer, need not prove anything for him to be acquitted. The prosecutor must prove beyond a reasonable doubt that the accused did what he is accused of doing. If the prosecutor fails in that task, the defence need not do anything. Even if the prosecution succeeds initially, the defence need only poke enough holes in the prosecutor's case to raise a reasonable doubt in a judge's or jury's mind. Even if a judge or jury strongly dislikes the accused, or they *suspect* he's guilty of the charge, a judge or jury cannot find him guilty if there is a reasonable doubt of that guilt. Moreover, the accused must be proven guilty of the specific bad act, and that allegation must meet the strict guidelines provided by law for that specific charge.

Do innocent people still get wrongly convicted? Sure. Mistakes happen. People sometimes lie. Evidence is sometimes missed or even hidden. Still, the justice system is heavily stacked in favour of the accused to avoid innocent people being convicted, even if it means some guilty people go free. Therefore, an acquittal means the accused was *not found guilty* within the justice system, which is a long shot from being proven innocent. Some facts may sufficiently prove someone's innocence to most reasonable people, such as video of the accused somewhere other than the crime scene when the crime happened. But, *not guilty* does not equal *innocent* any more than *not riddled with cancer* equals *perfectly healthy*.

Was O.J. Simpson proven innocent of murdering his wife and her friend? Nope. He simply wasn't proven guilty. When the videotaped officers accused of beating Rodney King were acquitted of charges related to that, they were not proven innocent either. In the latter case, the jury was left to consider all the facts and circumstances of the case including a cop's duties, their job related challenges, and use of force guidelines for the Los Angeles Police. The jury may have disliked the officers and what they did but declined to find them guilty due to the nature of the evidence and the burden on the prosecutor to prove that those officers sufficiently crossed the legal line to be convicted. That too is a far cry from innocent.

Both court cases were heavily covered in the media, affected by racial overtones, and interpreted by various talking heads. Some people drew conclusions that led to heavy cheering in the Simpson case, and led to heavy and deadly rioting in the King beating case. So much for academic exercises.

The words *proof* (noun) and *prove* (verb) are often misunderstood. Other commonly misunderstood words include *fact, know, see, hear, study* (noun) and *impossible* as well as phrases such as *could not have* and *for sure.* These words, or the words that make up the terms, are clearly defined in any number of reputable dictionaries so why are they misunderstood? And what's the big deal if they are?

You are likely familiar with seeing a split television on news networks with flashes streaming across one part of that screen. As the word *flash* implies, these are brief glimpses of the news. Consider this news flash: *Researchers prove link between male pattern baldness and prostate cancer, says study.* This wouldn't be minor stuff. Nothing involving cancer is minor. If you are man with male pattern baldness, like me, you might wonder if it is true or you might surf the internet all night trying to find out. You might buy a truckload of Rogaine or book hair replacement surgery.

I made the flash up but such a study could easily happen. Many reputable studies indicate the existence of high testosterone levels among men with male pattern baldness *and* men with prostate cancer. Be that as it may, that does not *prove* that high testosterone levels *cause* male baldness or prostate cancer. Nevertheless, an argument could be made for that hypothetical theory. That is all that reputable studies are, arguments supported by evidence of some kind.

The best researchers want their studies challenged to see if they are correct in their findings. Few reputable studies claim to *prove* anything. Previous theories considered beyond challenge included the sun revolving around the earth and the earth being flat.

You needn't be a genius or *uber*geek to avoid conclusions based on my fake news flash or real news flashes you see. You need only know what "*a study*" and "*prove*" mean. What if a real study like my fake one actually exists? The news flash might be remarkably similar. That still wouldn't mean the study was flawed or the researchers sloppy. Researchers don't enter information onto news flash screens, poorly paid television employees do. How accurately he (or she) does that job depends on how much he reads, how many other tasks he does, how hung over he is, and any number of other variables we are unaware of. Research studies usually number in dozens and sometimes hundreds of pages so they cannot be accurately summarized into two or three lines.

We all know what the term *second hand* means and surmise that second hand information has at least one person between the source and us. With a news flash, the news might be second hand, fifth hand, or tenth hand. Some people depend on news flashes and newspaper headlines for their understanding of what's happening in the world. Unreliable or inaccurate though those sources are, they are still better than what many other people feast on.

Exhibit A: Starting in October of 2002, the Toronto Star newspaper ran a series of articles about racial profiling by Toronto Police officers. The main story focused on analyses of arrests records, the description how many of those people were described as having "black" skin, and a comparison of those results against census figures for the city. From that, the writers implied that the police in Toronto wittingly or otherwise practiced racial profiling, particularly with Afro-Canadian people. The details hardly mattered, such as that black males born in some Caribbean nations were reportedly over represented among arrests while black males of African birth were reportedly under represented.

Those who previously accused police of racial profiling took the articles as proof positive they were right. Those who rejected racial profiling as a regular or systemic occurrence in Toronto saw the articles as just another baseless shot at the police. After reading those articles in detail and hearing many opinions on both sides, something became clear to me. While some people on each side of this heated debate seemingly read the material, others who were equally vocal made only the vaguest reference to any facts whatsoever. A vast number of people on either side of the debate who I spoke with didn't read the articles at all.

Those who saw racial profiling everywhere felt vindicated, many because they *heard someone say* articles from a major Toronto daily *proved* it. Those who saw no racial profiling anywhere were equally ill informed and killed the messenger, the Toronto Star being seen by many police supporters as biased against the police. That equally few numbers on *either* side of the fence actually read the articles, or knew how the writers reached their conclusions, hardly mattered. By definition, both sides commenced shovelling poop.

A senior boss I had at that time used to say *the devil's in the details.* As Professor Ron Melchers of the University of Ottawa pointed out in *Do the Toronto Police Engage in Racial Profiling*, his review of the Toronto Star-sponsored analyses, arrest records capture information from *incidents* whereas a census counts *people*. John Smith counts as one tick in a census but he could have been arrested seven times, accounting for seven ticks in arrest records. Melchers identified that kind of comparison as a *base error*. I refer to it as comparing apples to airplanes. Yet police advocates shouldn't rejoice. As with any acquittal, the Star's failure to prove anything did not disprove their claim or clear the police, as Melchers pointed out as well.

How did most people *learn* about the newspaper articles in question? They heard about it from someone else who heard from someone else and so on. People who would otherwise suspect something they heard third-hand accepted as gospel what they may have heard *twenty third* hand.

If you're not familiar with Broken Telephone, it's an old party game. You sit in a circle and whisper a sentence to someone to one side of you, who whispers what he heard to the next person and so on. When the person on your other side receives the whispered message, he says out loud what he heard, then you say out loud what you first said, after which laughter usually commences. If you said

"I keep my Pez dispenser in my bedroom overlooking the ocean", the end result might be "I dress my blue bed to see you", since oral information can often become garbled as it is repeated. That may not seem funny to you, but you're probably sober right now. Yet what a few drunks do for laughs other people seem to do all the time to get information, upon which they form their beliefs and decisions. Woo hoo, party on!

Should we reject anything we don't hear or read from the original source? There's a short and a long answer.

The short one: No.

The long one: We must ask a few questions and use our language skills, which improve with learning, practice, and thought.

Let's say a friend suggested you should drink lots of alcohol because people in France do and they have very low rates of heart disease despite high cholesterol diets. This might seem like BS, more so if the friend was a drunkard who hated to drink alone. Here's the problem, though: this particular poop dropping is typical in that it is not wholly false. As with lots of BS, there might be something of value to be sifted from the steaming heap.

The key is to ask questions. A good start is to find out where or from whom the information came. Was it the New England Journal of Medicine or Frank, the drooling guy in the corner? Was it his family doctor or his barber? Was it from his own travels to France or listening to a stand-up comic, whose stock and trade is BS for entertaining people? Finding the source can be a great indicator of how much effort should go into the sifting process. Other questions could address details of the information. Does any kind and amount of alcohol help or only a small amount of a certain kind?

Most BSers do not respond well to inquisitive questions since they either don't know the truth or they care what it is. Your BSer might not know where his information came from. Maybe he just heard it from a guy somewhere, some time ago. Maybe it made sense since his grandfather drank like a fish and lived until he was 92 years old, when he was run over by a truck. Never mind that the old guy stumbled in front of the truck while he was hammered. Most BS doesn't hold up well to even the most basic queries.

Those people least interested in poop sifting greet questions with scorn or ridicule. They sometimes cut you off (from the conversation, not the booze). By comparison, those with even a passing interest in facts might greet questions with honest responses and curiosity. "Come to think of it, I don't know, but I'd like to find out." Another way to sift through a pile is to ask other people some questions, perhaps medical professionals, or do your own research.

By recognizing BS when it arises but acknowledging there might be something useful in it, we can find a few welcome surprises. In fact, France is reported to have remarkably low rates of heart disease despite high fat diets *and* high smoking rates. Medical research *suggests* that a glass of red wine each day can help lower bad cholesterol levels. Knocking back a dozen beers every other day is another story. Don't take *my* word for it. Look it up.

Of course, language skills can avert any number of interpersonal troubles too. How many times does a person pass on something that isn't news or hard information, rather a version of what someone else said or did? This is the stuff of rumours and gossip, which are not confined to teenaged girls with overworked cell phones. Given how messed up hard facts and news can be mutilated in a poop chain, imagine how messed up less formal information can be, even when there is no bad intent on the part of those passing it on.

"He said what? She did what? Really? What a horrible girl!" Is there a question there, an actual query? More-useful questions would sound like this, "Who said that?",

"How do you know?", "When (or where) did she supposedly do that?" Once again, those with an interest in the truth will answer as best they can. Those with little interest in the truth will simply shrug, after which you can often ignore what was said.

If your approach to sifting involves running it by someone else, are you sifting a pile or just passing it on? BSers present poop as truth whereas more-honest folks run it by someone else with a warning that what follows *might* be BS.

Does all this talk of language scare you or bore you? Does it sound like a lot of mental work? It isn't. There are lots of games where the objective is to win or dominate an opponent yet there are other games you just play for fun, where you might learn something or you might get something out of it beyond momentary entertainment. Author Clyde Miller offered some advice concerning propaganda, a common form of BS:

> In examining these devices, note that they work most effectively at those times when we are too lazy to think for ourselves, also, they tie into emotions which sway us to be 'for' or 'against' . . ." Tying into emotions can be fun and harmless, such as when we watch a movie and cheer for a character that doesn't really exist or when we cheer for our team like our future depends on them winning. At other times, thought can be very important as well as fun too.

As Miller went on (and as quoted in the Introduction),

> With our emotions stirred, it may be fun to be fooled by these devices, but it is more fun and infinitely more to our own interests to know how they work.

Language is the gateway to reasoning, BS busting, and the fun associated with both. In *Your Call Is Very Important To Us, the truth about (BS)*, author Laura Penny also linked language and BS, "When people do not learn to read and write, and cannot own and operate their own language, then they are that much more susceptible to (BS)." Penny instructed junior college students in English. She explained that many students at that level required fundamental instruction in English despite graduating from various secondary schools. I know university professors in Canada and the United States who echo that frustration. Post-secondary education can be an enlightening and life changing experience yet there is no guarantee that a degree equips one to own and operate language effectively, much less reason effectively.

I believe the key to this owning and operating is an interest in precision. Ask lots of questions: "What does that word *mean*?" "Do you mean . . . ? "Why is that?" Oh yeah, and think! Post-secondary education can help you to learn about precision but so can reading books or listening to radio shows. So can thoughtful conversations with thoughtful people. So can watching thoughtful, detailed news shows from time to time. Don't worry, there's nothing wrong with lighter fare in between.

As foreign as this concept is to some people, learning can be fun and it can happen all the time. Ideally, as many adult education researchers state, we should all embrace life-long learning. Being the smartest kid in the class or the smartest adult in the meeting room is not the objective. A short sequence in the film *In the Line of Fire* illustrated this. Clint Eastwood's character met with fellow Secret Service agents about an anonymous bad guy who called him on his home phone the previous night, saying he would kill the President. Eastwood's character referred to the bad guy using the word *panache* and he began to explain what the word meant. As he did, his supervisor cut him off. "I know what *panache* means." She says.

"Really," Eastwood smiled, "I had to look it up."

I've had to look up a lot of words, some complex and little-used, many simple and often-used. I'm in my late 40s and nowhere near finished learning. Have you finished learning?

REASONING

This is where the rubber hits the road in terms of BS busting. Whether called critical thinking or something else, reasoning is a type of thinking. Many people believe they know how to think. I disagree in some ways and provide my reasoning for that momentarily.

Forget about thought for a moment and consider physical movement instead. With the exception of people unable to move due to a serious medical condition or physical disability, we all have the ability to move. It is an instinct with which we develop all sorts of other abilities over time. We learn to walk when our muscles develop sufficient muscular strength and coordination, when we have frequently seen other people walk, and after we've tried and failed many times over before walking slowly. Therefore, walking is an instinct most of us master with very little assistance, sooner or later.

How about ballet dancing or playing baseball? Certainly, some people can perform either on their own if they are very observant, and if they are dedicated enough to watch others do it, practice the required skills, correct their own errors, and have the courage to try and fail, perhaps many times over. While either achievement is remotely possible, becoming a ballet dancer or baseball player without proper guidance is very difficult.

Instincts are learned through time with self-driven practice. Skills usually require training or teaching, particularly to do them well. The mere ability to move does not allow you in and of itself to drive a car, fly an airplane, swim, or perform other physical skills.

Just as there are many types of movement there are also many types of thought, which can also be referred to as *processes.* There is language-based thought, mathematical thought, artistic thought, lateral thought, and many other kinds. There are also instinctive emotional reactions such as anger, fear, joy and anxiety, none that require any training whatsoever. Training is often required to help people *control* negative emotions such as fear and anger. Therefore, expecting someone to reason simply because he can talk, respond, and apparently perform *some* kinds of thinking is no more fair or *reasonable* than throwing that person on stage to dance in the Nutcracker Suite.

Why can some people think mathematically, speak another language, or perform other intellectual processes that other people cannot? Generally, many types of thought are formally taught in school, informally taught at home, or both yet many factors impact on how well a person learns thinking skills. They include parents' knowledge and interest in teaching particular skills, how effective a student's teachers are, how much they pay attention, how healthy their diet and sleep are. Even without formal education in some thinking skills, most people have a fighting chance to learn and even master some of them. That is fortunate because reasoning is rarely taught in explicit ways in elementary or secondary grades, nor is it mandatory in most university programs despite regular references to such intellectual characteristics as *criticality.* There are courses in critical thought available in some schools, and books on the topic available in bookstores and libraries. Nevertheless, you must know a skill exists before you can consider seeking training or knowledge in it.

There exists with any skill a four stage learning paradigm: (1) Unconscious incompetence, (2) conscious incompetence, (3) conscious competence and (4) unconscious competence. To start off with, we don't know what we don't know; if we are unaware that a particular skill exists we are incompetent at it but don't know that (1). Once we become aware of a particular skill, that knowledge doesn't provide us with the skill but makes us aware of our incompetence in it (2), which we can fix through learning and work if we choose to, and if we have the opportunity to learn. If we learn and practice, we develop the skill within ourselves to the point that we are competent in it and know that we are (3). As long as we keep practicing or performing the skill, we can improve at it to such a degree that we will no longer be consciously aware of performing the skill well (4). That happens in part because our consciousness moves on to other skills we are incompetent in, and partially because the human brain changes structure to allow us to do so with minimal conscious effort. Walking, riding a bicycle, driving, and speaking are examples of where you demonstrate this paradigm, perhaps daily. What initially takes work and thought becomes seemingly automatic, not to mention easy.

For this reason, I don't bother with finger pointing or blame when it comes to anyone who may lack reasoning skills, much as I wouldn't blame someone for not knowing how to fly an airplane, unless he or she is the pilot for my flight.

How does any or all of this relate to BS busting? Consider these questions:

- If a man had cow manure on his farm and wanted you to eat some, would you?

- What if he was a friend of yours?
- What if he gave it to someone who gave it to someone else, the manure passing through so many hands that you had no idea where it came from?
- What if many other people, millions perhaps, ate manure regularly?
- What if the praises of manure eating were printed in newspapers?
- Are there any circumstances whereby you would eat cow manure?

Ridiculous as those questions seem, let's take them a step further:

- If this poo peddler ran a company that put manure into delicious milk shakes, would you drink them once you learned the true ingredients?
- What if his company changed the flavour, packaging or advertising of his poo shakes?
- What if celebrities drank his poo shakes?
- Again, would any of this make any difference?

Do these questions seem stupid to you? Many people, perhaps most, consume a steady diet of BS, which thrives when people fail to notice it. Reasoning allows us to recognize BS and reveal it to others. Because reasoning is so rarely taught to people in a structured manner, a deficit in that skill reaches across social, cultural, racial, political, and economic boundaries, far more than deficits in well-known skills such as math and sciences. I'll give you an example I saw.

In 2010, Toronto hosted the G20 Summit, which drew many protesters. Most protesters were reasonable and non-violent but a minority were violent and destructive. After a day when police cars were burned, windows smashed, people attacked, and other nonsense carried out by people who often hid their faces with bandanas or masks, police changed their approach. They asked people attending rallies *and* wearing bandanas on their necks to do one of two things, surrender those bandanas until the summit was over, or provide their particulars so they could later be identified by their clothing and bandana if they were video recorded while committing crimes.

When officers approached two women wearing bandanas, and they explained the above points, one uninvolved protester jumped forward and started yelling, "That's a *fallacy*!" If you're not familiar with the term, and you soon will be, a fallacy is an error in reasoning, dozens which have been identified over many centuries. Unbeknownst to the officers or the women involved, the exchange was recorded and shown on CNN an hour later. When the officers ignored the woman they *weren't* speaking with, she repeated her claim several more times, after which one officer turned to her, "Which one? Name the specific fallacy."

She responded, "Look, I've been a debater, so I know a fallacy when I hear one."

"And I've taught critical thinking," the officer responded, "so precisely which fallacy are you referring to. *Non-sequitor*? *Argumentum ad hominem*? What?" The woman then withdrew into the crowd. The woman seemed well spoken, claimed to have debated previously, and perhaps had done so. She may have more educational credentials than the officer did. Still, who carried the day? The woman appears to have tried to baffle someone she thought she could, mistakenly as it turned out.

It is said that *BS baffles brains*. In truth, it only baffles *unprepared or unengaged* brains. The officers provided an easy-to-explain reason for their request of the other women, who cooperated. The yelling lady appeared to toss out a term to intellectually intimidate or embarrass the cops, but the officers were not committing any fallacies and at least one of them knew it. Even if the yelling woman may have known in other times and places that what she said was untrue, she may not have realized that or cared during her excited exchange with the two cops. Hence, it was not necessarily a lie but definitely untrue; it was BS.

Perhaps the officer had not previously taught critical thinking. Perhaps the weird-sounding terms he came up with were made up on the spot, or maybe he studied Latin as a kid. Be that as it may, simply calling the woman on her BS sent her packing. Such is the nature of most poop piles, that very little challenge of it is required to blow it up, usually all over those who shovel it. The best device to blow such piles up is *reasoning*.

Having sung the virtues and value of reasoning, let's take a cursory look at what it is. First consider the following definitions, abbreviated by me from common dictionary sources (I invite readers to confirm if they like):

- **Logic:** The flow and management of information, and drawing conclusions from it.
- **Reason:** (noun) A cause, or sanity. (verb) To think logically, with cause, sanely.
- **Critical** (commonly understood with several meanings): Dangerous (the situation is critical), life threatening (her injuries are critical), significant (a critical stage of the project), unfavourable (he was critical of my performance) and analytical (take a critical look at my plan).
- **Critic:** Someone who puts something or someone down consistently (such as a critic of one political party or view), or one who reviews something (such as a movie critic).
- **Critique:** (from French) An assessment, analysis, appraisal, or review.

There are many ways to process information. For instance, computers process data (mathematical information), which is why the traditional function of computers was first called *data processing*. Contrary to popular belief, computers are not intelligent, mostly because they have no brains. They can only perform the simplest math functions, adding and subtracting. If you want a computer to multiply 4 by 5, a computer programmer must instruct the machine to add 5 plus 5 and repeat that three times. A computer's charm is how fast it can execute instructions and the detail residing within those instructions. Thus, with incredible speed and by using programs made by humans, computers can perform very complex tasks. Those instructions are based in applied logic. The instructions in computer programs break a complex task into a series of much simpler ones.

If I asked you what 6 times 8 is, you would probably know the answer because you remember your multiplication tables. If I asked you, however, what 728 times 45 is, that would require you to perform a mathematical function. A calculator is merely a computer with various mathematical functions programmed into it. You punch in the numbers and choose the function, and then it processes those numbers in a specific logical way to produce the correct answer, 32,760 in the case of the above problem. It doesn't matter if you work it out yourself or use a calculator several times over, the answer will be the same each time because logic doesn't change. Logic doesn't apply one day and not the next.

In ancient Greece, some thoughtful people worked out specific ways of solving intellectual problems with ideas, just as others did the same with mathematical problems. In both cases, logic was required and no amount of time or change of scenery has modified logic in well over 2,500 years.

Does that mean whatever was believed back then is true today? Not at all. Consider the earlier examples of mistaken beliefs, of the world being flat and at the centre of the universe. Both beliefs were proven false, not with new logic but more information and logical processing of that. Newer arguments resulted from that information and processing, after which truth emerged. Authorities of the day tried to condemn those people who challenged the old beliefs, but truth is tough to silence forever.

As luck or knowledge would have it, the two Latin terms the cop in my earlier tale mentioned to the shrieking woman *are* fallacies. Latin is traditionally used to describe some fallacies because it was used in higher education in many European countries for centuries and because the terms are shorter than lengthy explanations of them. Of course, Europeans didn't corner the logic market. Some of them merely worked at describing that area of thought while people in other regions went about mastering other tasks.

The key aspect of logic that applies to reasoning is *flow*. There is a flow in the steps that collectively solve a given math problem. *If* the problem is 63 times 87,564, *then* you multiply the two numbers using the process for doing so. *If* the problem is finding the circumference of the pipe under your sink, *then* you use a different mathematical process. Reasoning is very similar.

As the definitions above show, reason and sanity are often very similar. If a woman walked up to you and said she was a Roman centurion, information at your disposal would not add up in a logical way to support that belief. If she was speaking English, that would be clue because the English language didn't exist until many centuries after the Roman Empire fell. She would not likely be dressed as an ancient Roman soldier. Ancient Rome collapsed about a millennium and a half ago, long before this woman would have been born no matter how many face lifts she may have had. And, the Romans didn't use woman as soldiers. Even with a small amount of historical knowledge, you would know she was no centurion. Moreover, you could look up what a Roman centurion was so you accurately knew what she was claiming to be. You wouldn't consider this woman mistaken or unreasonable even though she would be both. You would consider her crazy, emotionally disturbed, perhaps delusional.

Imagine instead that a teenager walked up to you and said he was part of the B Block Posse because anyone important from his apartment building was part of that gang, and that the only people who would help him were his posse members. It would be unlikely that all people in his area were part of his gang or that there was no help available to youth in that building other than from a criminal gang. The teen's beliefs would be no more reasonable than the delusional centurion's but few would consider this misguided youth to be insane.

Who would be in more danger of a violent death, involvement in the justice system, or other serious problems, the non-centurion or the grossly-mistaken youth? *Insane* is a label often used to describe people who have malfunctions within their brain, most which are caused by unbalanced brain chemistry, brain injury, or severe emotional trauma. The term can also apply to people at risk of serious harm due to unreasonable thoughts, yet it is rarely used that way. Fortunately, training in reasoning can cure that problem for people with otherwise functional brains.

As for the term *critical*, it merely refers to examination, consideration, or weighing the merits of an argument (when it comes to reasoning). When you think critically you take a critical look at what is presented and examine that to see if it *adds up.* After that consideration, you can decide whether or not to accept what you were told as true, based on established processes. While that may appear complex and time consuming, practicing this skill makes it nearly as effortless as knowing that 6 times 8 equals 48.

A few additional definitions are needed in order to move on:

- **Argument:** An oral dispute between people, or a statement that includes a conclusion and the reasoning to support it (the second definition applies in reasoning).
- **Statement:** A thought expressed as a sentence, claiming something that is either true or false. Directions and commands are not statements because they are neither true nor false.
- **Premise:** A statement claiming to support a conclusion.
- **Conclusion:** A statement claiming to be supported by other statements known as premises (*premise* when there is only one).

There are two parts to a reasoned *argument*, (1) a *premise* or group of them and (2) a *conclusion*, which itself can provide support for other conclusions. A statement such as, "You are wrong", "He's a good guy" or "She's a tramp" are neither premises nor conclusions, merely statements that mean nothing in terms of reasoning. They are opinions at best, which everyone has plenty of whether or not those are true or accurate.

There is a structure to mathematical processes, which are also known as *formulas*. Whether working out what a times b is or the square root of 134, there are formulas proven over many centuries to yield accurate results. *Structures* exist and work well within reasoning.

There are three basic structures and one advanced. Depending on the structure of an argument, if some or all the premises are true, the conclusion flowing from that should also be true.

A **simple argument** has one premise supporting a conclusion. Example: *Brian was born in Canada; therefore, he is a Canadian citizen.* This argument presumes that anyone born in Canada is automatically a Canadian citizen. If the premise is true then the conclusion should be too. Another example: *I once saw Ben knock a guy right off his feet, so he's a violent criminal.* Once again, if I'm telling the truth about what I saw Ben do, then my conclusion should be true too. If you believe the second argument is far from ironclad, you are correct. More on that later.

Symbols can be helpful in mathematics and flowcharts can be helpful in mapping complicated computer programs. In the same way, *argument trees* help people see the structure of an argument. The first diagram shows the argument tree of a **simple argument**.

A **T argument** gets its name from the shape made by the applicable argument tree (second diagram). Example: *When Jennifer was in the drug store, she put a perfume bottle from the cosmetic section in her purse. Then she walked out of the store without paying for it. Hence, Jennifer is a thief.* Both premises must be true for the conclusion to be true. If she didn't put any merchandise in her purse, Jennifer would have no reason to pay for anything. If she paid for what she put in her purse, then her actions would be a purchase.

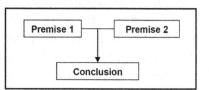

36

A **V argument** also gets its name from the shape of the applicable argument tree (third diagram). Example: *Yesterday I saw Rebecca fall down some stairs at work and today I saw her drop her cup of coffee on the ground. So she's obviously clumsy.* If either

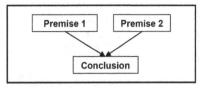

premise is true, the stair mishap or the dropped coffee, the conclusion *may* still be true, but if both premises are true then the conclusion is more likely true, it is more *probable*.

A **complex argument** (fourth diagram) differs from the basic forms in that at least one premise is also a conclusion, which then serves as a premise for a final conclusion. Example: *Brian was born in Canada therefore he is a Canadian citizen, so he is allowed to vote in Canadian federal*

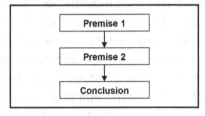

elections. At first glance, a complex argument need not be that complex, as the tree diagram seen right makes clear.

Nonetheless, complex arguments can be much more deserving of the term. Example: *Michelle, your boyfriend has two children by two different women, and he doesn't support them or their mothers in any way. So he's irresponsible and undependable. He has no skills and no job so it's unlikely he'll get a job in the foreseeable future. He's so lazy he doesn't even wash regularly. So, your boyfriend is irresponsible and undependable, he's unemployable, and he's dirty, so I don't think you should go out with him any more.* The tree for that argument would look like this:

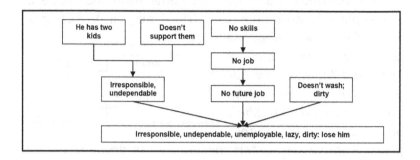

The structures listed above merely provide the basics of reasoning. An argument can *appear* true yet not be true at all. That's why reasoning doesn't necessarily stop with a single argument being posed. Nevertheless, reasoning provides a framework for considering and expressing ideas as well as a means of challenging them and learning from them. Arguments are rarely absolute in truth or accuracy.

In reasoning, there is a language tool that alerts people to a series of statements being related to one another, *the inference indicator.* Examples include *therefore, so, hence, thus, consequently, accordingly,* the semicolon (;), and several others. An inference indicator tells readers or listeners that the sentences are related to one another in a logical way. For example, if you said you were expelled from school and you were upset, you would be expressing two thoughts that may or may not be related. You might have been expelled because you were upset and did something harmful that resulted in your expulsion, or you might be upset about something unrelated to your expulsion. However, if you said you were expelled, *therefore* you were upset, your being upset would be clearly connected to your expulsion.

Quite often, people describe an oral dispute as an argument. It is, but that kind shouldn't be confused with a reasoned argument, which can be part of a reasoned dispute, whether oral or written. Another term for a reasoned dispute is *debate,* which is often associated with formal debate in an academic or political setting. Other terms for such exchanges or clash of ideas include *public debate* and *discussion.*

In debates and discussions, arguments are often responded to by *counterarguments*. It doesn't matter whether these are formal debates or informal discussions. This is far from the is-so/is-not nature of childlike arguments. It is also different from the more civilized and yet no more reasoned stance of some opposing adults, who *agree to disagree.* In constructive discourse, participants want to know the truth of what they discuss, so a discussion is a contest between ideas, not people. A counter argument is merely an argument that challenges an initial argument. Sometimes a counterargument will rip the first one to shreds, other times it will reveal a minor flaw, and other times it won't reveal any flaw whatsoever. Since constructive discourse is about truth finding, there are no losers if the truth is revealed.

This is precisely the way that ideas are posed, challenged, even changed sometimes. That process happens within many groups, the scientific community being just one. When someone publishes a study, that document is posed as a *thesis* that is published so it can be reviewed and potentially challenged by others in the same field. This process is known as *peer review*.

For instance, a medical researcher might publish a study suggesting that proximity to major highways can cause lung cancer based on data linking the two over a ten year period in one location. In the course of peer review, another researcher might pose an *antithesis,* if he found fallacies or factual errors in the initial thesis. Another researcher might repeat the same study with a slightly different approach, trying to replicate the same results. If the second study netted the same results, the second researcher would publish a supporting thesis and the initial theory would gain strength. If the results were different, the second researcher might publish an antithesis challenging the first theory. In any case, researchers would collectively move toward the truth of whether or not highway traffic causes a type of cancer.

Although discourse in medical research can take months, years, or decades, the very same process can take place between people within minutes, hours or a few days. Although far less scientific or studied, that is how many of us come to believe what we do.

Picture that an imaginary guy had very sore feet from standing on them all day as part of his new job, and that he brought that up during dinner conversation with friends. Our guy might tell his friends that he might have to quit his job over pain in his feet. One of other guys at dinner could be a construction worker who told our guy about foot problems he had until he bought a good pair of work boots. Another dinner companion might hike a lot and have told our guy how important good socks and arch supports were. A third friend might have sat on his backside all day at work and at home but surfed the internet on his smart phone so he had something to throw into the mix. After some back and forth between friends, some of them might make decisions based on that informal chat. Our guy with the sore feet might have then bought better work boots or socks. The construction worker might have later bought better socks the next time he was out shopping. That's how day-to-day reasoning usually works. The better at reasoning even one person in such a conversation is, the more likely the resulting beliefs will be true and maybe even helpful. Why quit a job over something that could be solved with better socks?

People who use reason want to find truth and accuracy. That is why it is important for us to have ways to assess how truthful or not a particular conclusion is. The aspect of an argument that makes its conclusion more or less likely to be true is *strength.* The conclusion of a strong argument is more likely to be true, and more probable, than that of a weak argument. Two facets of an argument determine the relative strength of it: the *truth* of the premises and the *soundness* of the argument, the latter which is often more useful to assess.

"Hold on!" you might now think, "When you want to know what is true or not, why not focus on *truth*?" Sensible though that seems, figuring out what premises are true or not is often a lot more difficult than assessing the soundness of the argument as a whole.

Consider this argument: *Black people are five times more likely to have unplanned babies than other racial groups, so the police should watch black people more carefully when on patrol.* If you are disgusted by the argument, you should be regardless of what racial group you identify with. This argument shows why reasoning is so important. Reasoning is not only required in classrooms or intellectual discussions, it is needed in day-to-day conversations among people of all walks of life and ethnic groups. This last argument partially shows why.

Without reasoning skills, one might reject the argument simply because he doesn't *want* the conclusion to be true. Conversely, he might accept it simply because he believes it is true, perhaps out of an existing racial bias. If this argument were posed in the media, thousands of people might line up on either side of that argument, some rejecting it out of hand and others accepting it with no more thought than the first group. How much closer would we be to the truth of that issue? Not an inch.

Reasoning works best when we all step aside from our emotions and biases. Almost all of us have plenty of both, whether we admit it or not. Then it is much easier to find the truth, or lack of it, in the arguments we come across. With a reasoned eye, let's examine the repulsive argument above.

At first glance, the argument may appear simple in structure, but it isn't. If you recall, an argument has a conclusion supported by one or more premises so there must be a flow *from* a premise *to* the conclusion for the latter to stand. *If* the premise in a simple argument is true *then* the conclusion should also be true. Structural integrity is what makes an argument sound. If an argument isn't sound, it doesn't matter whether or not any premise is true because there is no logical connection between the two.

There is no logical connection between how likely or not people in a particular racial group are to have unplanned babies and how police should do their jobs. Even if the premise were true, the argument would be weak. Sure, it is repulsive to decent people's emotions but it is also extremely weak to the reasoned mind, no matter what biases that mind may have and no matter the colour of skin wrapped around the cranium which holds that mind.

As it happens, I made up the premise out of thin air. How would you know that, though, unless you were an expert on current statistical studies or spent hours surfing reliable internet sources for such a study? With a basic understanding of reasoning, you could dismiss the racist argument in seconds, not out of bias or even decency, rather out of logic and efficiency. With that extra time, you could tell other people what a BSer or maybe even racist the source of such a weak argument was.

Another aspect of assessing the soundness of an argument is assessing the credibility of the source. For instance, the racist argument above is so weak that many reasonable people would doubt the accuracy of the premise because of that weakness. If someone is so unreasoned and intellectually weak, he might be too lazy to find true premises to use in his arguments too.

While *easy* and *simple* are not synonymous, they are sometimes complimentary. When it comes to assessing the strength of an argument, assessing the structure is often easier *and* simpler than lengthy fact checking.

Think back to the woman protester taking exception to the cops at a demonstration, the one who repeatedly yelled, *"That's a fallacy!"* By definition, a *fallacy* is an error in logic or reasoning. Put another way, it is an error in the structural integrity of an argument. Hence, an argument with a fallacy is *fallacious.* Dozens of fallacies have been identified over many centuries. Be that as it may, without identifying *which* fallacy the officers were committing in their V argument, the woman posed little more intellectual challenge than if she had stood there yelling, "Wrong, wrong, wrong!"

There are two ways to identify a structurally weak or invalid argument. One requires you to remember a list of (at least) the most-common fallacies and is called the *Fallacies Approach.* The other requires you to spot the absence of soundness in an argument based on certain criteria, which is called the *Criterial Approach.* Which one is better? Let's see.

There are over a dozen common fallacies and arguably dozens beyond that. Yet there are only four structures which provide soundness in reasoning, all of which we've already covered. By default, if an argument doesn't pass the sniff test that is the Criterial Approach, it deserves no more consideration beyond that.

Criteria are standards, so the criterial approach sets out a list of standards an argument must meet for it to be considered sound. There is a seven-step process to thoroughly assess that soundness, yet three of those criteria provide a handy set of filters for poop sifting: *acceptability, relevance* and *adequacy.*

If an argument is sound, its premises will be readily **acceptable** to a reasonable person.

Consider this argument: *I heard Jennifer has been with a lot of guys, so she is promiscuous.* How acceptable is my premise? Who did I hear that from? How accurate might that unnamed person's information be? What does *been with* mean? And what is *a lot* anyway? If my source is a Mennonite, Jennifer may have done nothing more than walk down the street with a different guy or two in her village. Besides, how can you check out the truthfulness or accuracy of my premise? Meanwhile, if you accept my argument then poor Jennifer could be unfairly branded.

Now compare it with this argument:

> According to the website Suite101.com *(July 23, 2010,* Clayton Browne, Bicycle Safety—Why Children Should Wear Bicycle Helmets), wearing helmets greatly reduces the severity of head injuries during bicycle accidents during which the rider's head strikes the bike or ground. Therefore, helmets should be made mandatory for all bicycle riders.

In this instance, I referred to the information of just one guy but I gave you a road map to find exactly what he said and his reasoning for why he said it. At a glance, this argument appears more acceptable *and* it is far easier to verify. Many acceptable premises will be properly sourced and easy to check. Weak premises will be so vague as to make it nearly impossible to verify one way or the other. Because a BSer doesn't care whether a premise is true or false, vague premises are a favoured tool for poop shovelling.

If an argument is sound, its premises will also be **relevant.** They will support the conclusion within one of the structures covered previously.

The racist argument I previously posed is an example. Whether or not the premise from that argument was true, it would not logically lead to the conclusion. There was no connection between the premise and the conclusion in that offensive argument except the mention of black people. Unplanned births are irrelevant to crime fighting, unless another argument provides a logical connection between the two.

If an argument is sound, its premises must also be **adequate.** The premises must provide enough support for an average, reasonable person to conclude the argument is true.

Consider this argument: *OJ Simpson hated his wife after she left him so he's the guy who murdered her.* Even if my lone premise was true, and it might be, would it adequately provide support for my conclusion? It might provide a motive for him killing his wife and her friend, but how was the murder done? Was Simpson able to carry that out? Where was he when these murders were committed? My singular premise was inadequate to support such an ambitious conclusion, even if my premise was true. If I instead said, *OJ Simpson hated his wife after she left him so he had a motive to kill her,* my premise would be far more adequate for the conclusion. That conclusion could serve as one of many premises within a complex argument for the more ambitious conclusion that he committed those murders.

When it comes to the criterial approach, the three criteria explained above filter BS much like an aquarium filter catches fish poop. Many fallacious arguments will be stopped dead in their tracks by how unacceptable the premises for them are. Even if the premises appear acceptable, they will fail because they are irrelevant to the conclusion. And, even if their premises appear acceptable *and* relevant, some arguments will fail because those premises are inadequate to support the conclusion.

The *Fallacies Approach* may seem more involved since you need to learn the most common fallacies if you want to recognize them when they pop up. Yet while there are many fallacies, the most common ones show up most often and reduce the list considerably. You have probably seen many of them yourself. Even if you don't yet know the terms for them, you may subconsciously recognize many. The most common fallacies were identified many centuries ago. After all, BS is an ancient problem.

As I explained previously, many fallacies are known by Latin terms because that was the popular language among European scholars for centuries. In addition, many Latin terms are shorter than the English explanation of them. A simplified list follows here including the Latin terms where they exist.

Undefined Terms or Abstractions: Many arguments fail because they don't properly define a topic. Example: *London, England is the greatest city in the world.* I have nothing bad to say about London, which is highly regarded and one of the best known cities on the globe. I grew up in the drizzle of Vancouver so I don't even have an issue with London's weather. Yet without determining what constitutes *greatness* for a city, this is a difficult argument to prove one way or the other.

This fallacy often results in useless bickering or pointless arguments because the parties in dispute do not properly understand what the other is talking about. Instead, each argues against what he or she *thinks* the other is saying.

Generalizations: Also known as ***dicto simpliciter*** (spoken simply), this fallacy makes sweeping statements, expecting them to be true in every specific case such as stereotyping. Example: *My husband hit me before I left him, so all men are violent.* Although the emotion behind such an argument would be understandable, the conclusion refers to every male on the planet, which may be a little broad. If the conclusion only referred to men who hit their wives or to one specific offender, it would be far more accurate and better defined. Certainly it would apply to this woman's husband. When generalizations are used, not only are there exceptions, sometimes the majority of cases defy those generalizations.

Antiquity/Tradition or Authority: An *argumentum ad antiquitatem* (argument to antiquity, thus tradition) and an *argumentum ad vericandium* (argument to authority) are different but related in one key element, their irrelevance.

An argument to tradition states that things have always (or for a long time) been that way so they always should be. Arguments to authority are often just as irrelevant. "Because I said so" is rarely accepted by the average teenager, let alone someone skilled at reasoning, and a well-known person's opinion on the matter may hold little more water, unless that person has expertise on the topic and that expertise is referenced in the argument.

Anecdotes and Sampling: Although these differ slightly, what makes them fallacies is the same. An argument using either is fallacious because they are stories or samples, not necessarily accurate representations that prove anything.

Example: *I went to Hawaii and had a terrible time, so no one should waste their time and money going there.* One person's experience can be similar to that of the majority or it can be unique. Without additional premises, there is no way to know. One small group can provide opinions consistent with the majority or completely out of touch with it. You may as well flip a coin as draw broader conclusions from the narrow experience or opinions of a few people, let alone one person.

Arguments to Numbers or the Public: An *argumentum ad numerum* (argument to numbers) or an *argumentum ad populem* (argument to the population, the public) solve the problems present in anecdotes and sampling, but neither makes a premise any more relevant.

Suppose someone says that two million music listeners can't be wrong in their favouring one musician over another. Sure they can. Centuries ago, most people in Europe believed diseases were the result of bad blood that had to be drained from the suffering person. The popularity of that belief didn't make it true and it was eventually proven false. Public opinion is sometimes correct and sometimes large numbers support reasonable conclusions, yet numbers or popularity will rarely support conclusions on their own.

Ignorance and Logic: Although completely different *words*, these two fallacies are similar in one regard. An ***argumentum ad ignorantiam*** (argument to ignorance) assumes something is true because it has not been proven false, at least to the knowledge of the person making the argument. Someone believes something is true simply because he doesn't know of it being proven false. Ignorant people rarely look for contradictory proof or they intentionally avoid it. So, even if an argument is made and not immediately countered, that doesn't make its conclusion true.

An ***argumentum ad logicam*** (argument to logic) is precisely the opposite, assuming something is false just because it hasn't been proven true. People looking for the truth actively seek it, even if someone else wasn't able to show it yet. Atheism is a good example of this fallacy. The absence of documented, concrete proof that God exists does not necessarily prove that He doesn't.

Circular Arguments or Begging the Question: *Circular in Demonstrando* (circular argument) uses the conclusion as part of the premises, stating the same thing in both and proving nothing. While the conclusion may be true, nothing in the premise supports it. Both the premise and conclusion are the same statement with varied words. Example: *Mr. Smith is so mean to students so he obviously hates them, which is why he's so mean to them.*

Petitioning or Begging the Question: *Petitio Principii* is a variation of circular arguments, assuming in the premises what one *pretends* to prove in his argument. Example: *Poor people and racial minorities do badly in school so the school system shouldn't waste time and energy trying to help them; they don't learn very much anyway.* If the performance of some students lags behind, that is certainly not established by this fallacious argument. Even if poor people or minorities actually lag behind by measurable standards, the very reason for such deficits may be a lack of help provided to those students, help which more-privileged-and-affluent students receive. The students who achieve higher marks may go to better-funded schools, enjoy better-supported sports and arts programs, and they may have less need for part-time jobs or other factors that can interfere with their school work.

Causation: There are two fallacies known as ***cum hoc ergo propter hoc*** (with this, therefore because of this) and ***post hoc ergo propter hoc*** (after this, therefore because of this). Each claims a relationship between incident and result simply because both occur closely in time or location.

Example: *Whenever football games are televised, more fist fights occur in bars so televised football games are the cause of drunken fist fights.* If a relevant link exists, a strong argument will include supporting premises. Without additional premises, this kind of argument relies only on coincidence.

No Flow: A *non sequitur* (does not follow) uses premises that do not logically follow the conclusion so they are irrelevant to it. The racist argument I posed earlier in this chapter is a good example. High rates of unplanned babies (within any identifiable group) do not necessarily lead to more crimes being committed by the youth or adults those kids later become.

Slippery Slope: This fallacy is a variation of the non sequitur. It occurs when an argument states that one result will lead to another without providing any logical flow between the two. Example: *Don't support Obamacare or we will be living in a communist state in no time.* This fallacy is often used to raise emotion or fear, which are the chief tools of propagandists and poop speakers. It is spotted exactly the same way a non sequitur is because there is no link between premises and prediction.

Arguing Off Point: Also known as *Ignoratio Elenchi* (ignoring the issue), or as a *Red Herring,* this fallacy is common and easy to spot. Arguing off the point brings up side issues that do not concern the main one being disputed. People often bring up side issues if the debate isn't going in the direction they prefer, or when they lose focus on the issue. It is logical and usually more effective to deal with one issue and *then* move on to another.

Straw Man: This fallacy occurs when someone opposing an argument doesn't refute it, only an extreme version of it. For that reason, it often shows up in counter arguments (antitheses) rather than the initial ones (theses).
This occurs when someone fundamentally misunderstands what the issue is, such as when undefined terms or abstractions are argued. It also occurs when someone intentionally presents an extreme version to trick someone else into substituting emotion for reason.

A common example of this is an oral dispute wherein one person accuses the other of *twisting his words*.

In an organized discussion of issues, this fallacy is easy to discredit by restating what was originally said. That clarifies your position and appeals to the other person's reason. If no reason is apparent, this is an argument you can't win. In fact, it may not be an argument at all, in which case further discussion is pointless and a waste of your time.

Directed Attack: This commonly-used fallacy is known by several names, most notably **name calling, argumentum ad hominem** (argument to person), or an **ad hominem attack**. It occurs when someone attacks the character or motives of a person posing an argument rather than attacking the argument itself. Like other propaganda devices, it is usually used to raise emotion and block reason.

Another way this fallacy is used is to assume something that is difficult to know much less prove: what someone else is thinking. Example: *He only wants your vote so he can close the local schools.* None of us knows exactly what anyone else thinks or believes unless that person explicitly tells us. Those who attack motives without supporting evidence imply that they know what their opponent(s) is thinking. How true or honest is that?

An occasional example of a directed attack is when one person suggests a similarity between someone with opposing views and Adolf Hitler, or the Nazis who followed that maniacal idiot. As a political pundit explained recently when talking about a new member of the Canadian parliament making such a comparison, the first one to mention Hitler usually loses in any debate.

Repetition: Also known as **argumentum ad nauseum** (argument to nausea, thus to the point of disgust through repetition), this fallacy states something repeatedly to convince someone of the truth of it. If an argument is weak, it is weak no matter how many times it is repeated.

False Analogy: *Finding a good mechanic and finding a good family doctor are similar because you need someone who is competent in either case.* That analogy doesn't compare the education or skill level of the two professions, merely the importance of having someone dependable and trustworthy to turn to in times of need. Therefore, it is an accurate analogy.

By comparison, *false* analogies can mislead people by bringing to mind familiar ideas in an attempt to transfer the truth of them to issues they don't accurately apply to. Example: *A good mechanic doesn't need nine years of school and training so a good doctor shouldn't either.*

Reasoning has its place in a variety of verbal circumstances. For instance, an argument need not start a conversation. It can be a response to a question. Consider the following hypothetical exchange:

Boss: Are you an idiot? Why didn't you send out the uniform order to Sutton Place Hotel? You know how important their business is for us.

Supposed idiot: Well, they didn't call us by Tuesday with all the sizes they need, like their guy in purchasing promised. The pants we ordered to make up their order are a different shade than what we already have in stock. And, the tailor had to go home because he has the flu. So I couldn't send the order out or it would be unfinished due to a lack of information and tailoring, and what I could send out wouldn`t match their existing uniforms.

Boss: Customers don't care *why* an order can't be filled. They only care about getting what they want when they want it.

Not so much an idiot: You're right, Boss. But I called the purchasing guy late yesterday to ask for the rest of the sizes. I waited to call until the end of the day so he couldn't expect the order yesterday or even today. Plus, he still doesn't have all the sizes and said he won't until tomorrow. So he doesn't even know we have a sick tailor, who will probably be back tomorrow anyway. I also sent the new pants back and the supplier promised me the right colour in two days, tops.

Boss: What if the purchasing guy gets back to you tomorrow with his sizes?

Smart employee: No worries, Boss. He knows tailoring takes a few days and he thinks he's the reason for the delay. He knows we have other business and a schedule to juggle. If he calls tomorrow with the sizes, and I don't think he'll have his act together by then, I'll say our tailor is tied up at the moment, which is true because he's sick, and we'll get his order done quickly despite the delay on their end. In the meantime, the tailor will already have half the order ready to ship by tomorrow evening anyway.

Boss: Do you really think that'll fly? They bring in a lot of business for us.

Genius employee: Not only will it fly, Boss. They'll think we went over the top to get their order done so quickly after all the delays on their end. Given everything that happened, it's a Godsend their purchasing guy is so unorganized. We caught a break and we'll shine because of it.

Boss: You're a good kid. I think I should look at you for shop manager when Smitty retires in July.

Without reasoning skills, the same scenario might play out like this:

Boss: Are you an idiot? Why didn't you send out the uniform order to Sutton Place Hotel? You know how important their business is for us.

Supposed idiot: (Gulp), Um, uh, geez Boss. I don't know what to tell you other than sorry. Um . . .

Boss: Sorry doesn't keep customers or pay the bills, Son. I'm really disappointed in you. I leave the shop for a few days when Smitty's away and, well, look at

	what I get for giving you a little trust.
Battered employee:	Hey it's not my fault . . .
Boss:	Always someone else's fault, eh? What are you, six? Maybe I advanced you too fast. I think you need a spell back in shipping.
Pissed-off employee:	Shipping?! After all I've done for this company? You don't even know what's going on here!
Boss:	I don't pay people to give me the same crap I get from my wife at home. Pack your desk, Kid. You're done here.
Former employee:	But, the purchasing guy didn't even give me all the measurements yet.
Boss:	You've said plenty, Kid. Get out!

There are two other aspects to thinking that are not part of reasoning but which can significantly affect the hunt for truth and accuracy. These aspects are evident in academic papers, in casual conversation, and in almost anything in between the two. Therefore, they bear mentioning and consideration.

Context: People love to repeat something that sounds good to them when someone else says it. In the Language chapter, I refer as an example to a woman who announced she was "losing her scruples", hopefully having no idea what that word meant. Another example of misunderstanding is when someone says their words were "taken out of context". I seriously question how many people who toss that term around truly understand what it means.

As you may know already, *context* is a set of circumstances or facts that surround an event. Without circumstances *and* facts, the truth of any matter can be missed or hidden or conveniently forgotten. That is why context is so often avoided by skilled BSers and why it bears so much on reasoning.

I saw one group of guys slaughter another last night. Am I a cold-hearted bastard or was something else at play here? Actually, it's *who* was at play, namely the New York Giants handily defeating the Minnesota Vikings in a Monday night football game. As another example, my second sample of a simple argument earlier in this chapter is completely without context: *I once saw Ben knock a guy right off his feet, so he's a violent criminal.* If Ben was on the street when I saw this, he may be a violent criminal. If he was playing hockey and knocked an opponent down, my conclusion could be wrong. I wouldn't be committing a fallacy or lying but by omitting the context, I would sure be shovelling something about Ben.

The context of a situation can sway the entire matter. News headlines, short claims, factually weak arguments, and brief accusations are often devoid of context. The absence of context can make it difficult to grasp what the truth is. On the other hand, someone without the slightest interest in the whole truth won't care about messy things like context.

Let's say you read this headline: *Teens caught on video struggling with man.* Some people might think, "Ah ha! Another bunch of young thugs caught red handed." Absent context, how could you possibly know what happened or who the bad guys really were? The video could have been the last fifteen seconds of a two-minute encounter. The teens may have randomly targeted some poor victim, or they may have been apprehending an offender who just attacked a victim. Details matter. Those are usually found within context.

Bias: This is essentially a prejudiced view of something. You might think that a conscious effort to remove bias from your examination for truth would take care of that. I used to believe that and I still do my best to be unbiased, but many instances arise when it may not be the case despite my best efforts. Unlike conscious prejudice, bias can be subconscious and much more difficult to recognize. When you cannot recognize a problem, it is difficult to fix. A very good habit for avoiding the effects of unconscious bias is to habitually employ reason. For example, many biased views will reveal fallacies, thereby revealing logical errors.

Not all bias is negative. Most parents are biased in favour of their children and all the positive things their kids do. On the flip side, that same bias can blind parents to their kids doing poorly or doing bad things.

Opinions in particular can be affected by all sorts of bias. Like many writers, I ask people to read earlier drafts of my work to get opinions on how that work reads, if it flows well and makes sense, if it is a fun or entertaining read, that sort of thing. This is commonly known as *feedback reading.* With that feedback, writers can change some parts of their work to achieve what they're trying to. Favourable bias can get in the way of the feedback I receive so I often choose people who I know will give me the straight goods. If my work sucks, I need to know that. Hopefully, my feedback readers didn't let me down with this book. I also have to choose people who are less likely to have a positive bias toward me as a person, so I rarely ask relatives or close friends to do feedback reading for me. In addition and for the same reason, I sometimes seek feedback readers who I barely know, and some who don't read much or even like to read. After all, if someone dislikes reading but enjoyed my work, I may be onto something.

A difficult type of bias to recognize is *confirmation bias.* We all have beliefs, some reasonable, some less so. Confirmation bias occurs when you examine a situation, *some* aspect of that fits into a bias you have, and you see that aspect as confirmation of your bias even if we are not conscious of it, and even if other aspects of the situation contradict that bias.

Bias in general, and confirmation bias in particular, pop up within many people, a great number who are probably decent on the whole. Still, bias is bias.

I recall hearing early news reports about a woman being brutally slain in a part of Toronto where I used to work, an area plagued by economic and social problems, including violent crime. When early news reports of the murder were aired, the news media released information that the unknown suspect was a male with black skin. The area where the murder occurred has a significant black population, many high profile crimes in the area have reportedly involved people with black skin as suspects *and* victims, and early media reports were consistent with that. So I imagine such media reports confirmed a bias in many people's minds.

Because I know one of the officers who attended that incident, I know that neither the victim nor her attacker had black-skin. I don't know where the mistaken information came from. Something else I don't know is how many potential witnesses didn't bother calling police about something they knew or saw because it wasn't about a "black man". Aside from a racial group being slammed within some subconscious or conscious minds, a murderer may still be walking around because of a bias within one or more news reporters.

Bias leads some people to see racism everywhere and others to see it nowhere unless the alleged perpetrator is wearing a white hood. Ironically, some people accuse everyone on the other side of their particular issue of being biased when they are no less biased, and possibly *more* biased. As with any other aspect of reasoning, it's not enough to *just know* a particular person is biased on any issue. It takes facts, details, and context to reason out whether or not any bias is creeping into a debate.

Is reasoning a purely academic exercise and of no use in the real world? You decide, after a little reasoning of course. I invite readers to challenge everything I write here. After instructing readers on reasoning and prodding them to use it, I don't expect a free pass here on what I tell them. I would be lying if I said that all I write here is bullet proof. Some of what I write may verge on BS, if only by accident. I'm happy to have my errors pointed out. Just do it gently because I'm very sensitive. No BS.

BENIGN DROPPINGS

I magine, if you will, arriving at someone's home for dinner. Let's call your host Glen. You have never been to Glen's before or eaten his cooking. When you arrive, Glen tells you he was running late, rushed cooking the roast, and is concerned it will be as tasty as dried up leather. He seems genuinely embarrassed, apologizing in advance for a meal he is sure will disappoint.

Being the kind, well-spoken guy or girl you are, out comes a courteous response most of us automatically spew, myself included: *Aw, don't worry Glen* (or whatever your host's name is), *I'm sure everything will be great.* Of course, this is BS of the highest order. Even if Glen had a Ph.D. in Applied Logic, though, he would likely accept your graciousness and serve dinner, whether it was a gastronomic wonder or inedible slop. Although he would *seem* to accept your assurance that everything would be fine, Glen could not possibly believe it because you could not possibly know how something would turn out in his kitchen. Glen accepting your assurance would, then, also be a form of BS. So why would you get a pass for BSing and Glen get a pass for letting that slide? After going over some important tools for detecting, challenging, and eradicating poop speak from our lives, how could we give you and that kitchen disaster of a friend a pass on BSing?

In terms of analogy, opium and BS share some parallels. Opium grows within opium poppies and is the basis for a range of very-strong drugs, some illegal, some legal, and some legally-produced but illegally abused. Opium-based drugs are the most-effective ones known to counteract serious pain. They include oxycontin and morphine as well as heroin. Even lawfully-prescribed pain medications with opium are highly addictive, which is why responsible physicians are so cautious about prescribing them and diligent in monitoring patients' use of them. Doesn't opium sound like dangerous stuff, the kind that should be banned from use by anyone? Yes and no.

There is a legitimate need for opium-based products. Many patients recovering from serious surgeries or battling advanced-stage illnesses would suffer unbearably without these products. To deny such people pain relief would be cruel and more harmful than any problems associated with use of those medications. Hence, opium is helpful and necessary stuff in small amounts and in specific circumstances under watchful control. The rest of the time, opium is really bad news.

There are proper uses for opium but they are in the minority compared with all the abuse of legal opium medications and illegal opium-based drugs. The same can arguably be said for alcohol, caffeine, sugar, animal fat in one's diet (although vegetarians and vegans disagree), and so on. None of these are wholly bad yet overuse can and does cause terrible problems. The same can be argued for firearms. Some people love them, others hate them, yet even those who hate them probably approve of certain people having them, such as their country's soldiers and police officers when bad guys are crossing their borders or approaching their kids. There are circumstances where a prudent amount of BS helps, kind of like sprinkling actual cow manure on the vegetable garden versus plopping it on the dinner table. I refer to these small helpings as *benign droppings.*

Benign is often seen as the opposite of cancer because it is the opposite of *malignant,* a term often taken to mean *cancerous.* If the doctor finds an abnormal growth within a patient, everyone hopes it will be revealed through pathology as *benign*, usually meaning harmless. Benign BS is that which is harmless, but it is also much more. *Benign* is synonymous with *caring* and *kind. Brutal honesty* is everything the term suggests. Sad to say, I've been guilty of its use from time to time. There are circumstances when honesty is called for no matter how brutal it is and other times when a benign sprinkling of BS may be just what the doctor ordered, so to speak.

Let's look at the alternative to benign BS as it would apply to Glen's impending dinner disaster. In response to his just-in-case apology, imagine that you didn't dish out any BS whatsoever, that you blurted out whatever came to your mind. Here are some possible examples:

- *If you hadn't rushed so much you wouldn't have that problem.*
- *Why not toss it out and we'll get take out instead.*
- *Great, now you made a* you *problem into a* we *problem.*
- *I rearranged my whole week for this dinner and you can't get your act together in your own home. Oh yeah,* that's *fair* (add sarcastic tone for effect).

Do any of these options seem preferable? They might feel good for a split second, until the evening turned into an awkward stare off for all involved. Besides, would you *know* Glen's dinner would suck? For that matter, would he? Even if his dinner sucked by *his* standards, Glen might be an amazing chef whose standards are quite high compared to yours. Tasteless slop to one person may be a great feast to another.

It helps here to remember the difference between the more effort filled lie and the effortless helping of BS. In the dinner scenario, you couldn't know you were wrong in advance, not for sure. And, would you care if you were right? Salvaging the evening and some possible friendship is often preferable to brutal honesty, which could turn out to be incorrect anyway. Given the context of that imaginary scenario, the most reasonable course of action might be to dish out a small helping of you-know-what.

I don't suggest you huddle up with friends in advance for the best response to a guy apologizing for a possibly poor dinner. Nor do I suggest detailed analysis of your verbal options before responding. Besides, many of us are unaware of the lightning-fast thought processes which occur in our brains, a topic covered in detail in Malcolm Gladwell's *Blink*. My point is to show that benign BS can withstand scrutiny and critique when it occurs. That is in stark contrast to other forms of BS that contribute to all sorts of bad results, and which I address in the next chapter.

Moving on from Glen's home, let's look at other instances of benign BS. You may have shovelled similar bits yourself. Let's say a three-year-old child showed you her latest artistic creation. You would likely tell the little angel how beautiful the picture was. The alternative would be to tell a little girl her work was infantile or no better than a gorilla might do. Since you are probably not a bastard or a witch, you would skip that alternative. Yet there might be other reasons to go with Option A. A few rough lines and misplaced colour may seem infantile to an adult, but it is unreasonable to expect more from a three-year-old human. At that age, a child's brain development, hand-eye coordination, and other abilities are just beginning to emerge. If the artist were a twenty-year old woman with a considerable developmental deficit, it might still be unreasonable to expect Rembrandt-like work from her. In context, the artistic work might be fantastic and your comment far from BS.

Most people don't bother with such considerations before heaping praise on children, for anything from pooping in the right place to getting their food in the correct orifice. That's good because children need and deserve encouragement. When that praise comes without consideration, it might be BS but only the best-intended and most-benign kind.

Let's say a wife asks her hubby or boyfriend, perhaps both at different times, if a particular garment makes her look fat. This familiar mind field has scared many a socially stupid man, including me. The usual response is safe and simple: "No", preferably without a microsecond of hesitation. As with so many benign examples, little or no thought goes into the truth of the matter. Yet even if thought *did* go into the denial, would it be untrue? Like *good, bad, stupid* and other judgmental words, the adjective *fat* is a relative term. Someone who a ballerina considers fat might be considered skinny by a shot putter. Many men and woman prefer differing body types in their mates, some wanting relatively thin, others relatively *festive*. Even if a significant other gained weight since the relationship began, that could still be within what her partner considered acceptable and well short of the other dreaded F-word. Then, of course, there's the whole matter of loving someone for far more than their physical characteristics. Sparing someone's feelings may well be within the realm of truth even if some thought was put into the answer.

These examples share a commonality that I suggest is the aspect of thought which sets us apart from all other species. What makes us special in comparison to other creatures, at least in our own minds? It is not opposable thumbs, which several primates and other species have. It isn't three-dimensional vision, which almost any species with both eyes pointed in the same direction have. As a general rule, predators share this trait so we can judge the distance of prey; most species lower in the food chain have eyes pointed out to their sides to better spot predators, nature or God being sporting after all. So what makes us different? It is as plain as the nose on your face and just a bit north of there.

Many neurologists believe that what makes us different is the part of the brain guarded by our forehead. Dogs', cats', squirrels' and primates' heads slope straight from the top of their skulls to their eyes whereas we have this chunk of brain in front that requires a much-differently shaped skull. Different portions of the brain are referred to as *lobes.* The area guarded by your forehead is sensibly called the *frontal lobe.* In *Stumbling on Happiness,* Harvard psychologist Daniel Gilbert discussed the importance of the frontal lobe and how mankind first glimpsed its function:

> Until fairly recently, scientists thought it was not much good at all, because people whose fontal lobes were damaged seemed to do pretty well without them. Phineus Gage was a foreman for the Rutland Railroad who, on a lovely autumn day in 1848, ignited a small explosion in the vicinity of his feet, launching a three-and-a-half-foot-long iron rod into the air, which Phineus cleverly caught with his face. The rod entered just beneath his left cheek and exited through the top of his skull, boring a tunnel through his cranium and taking a good chunk of frontal lobe with it. Phineus was knocked to the ground, where he lay for a few minutes. Then, to everyone's astonishment, he stood up and asked if a coworker might escort him to the doctor,

insisting all the while that he didn't need a ride and could walk by himself, thank you. The doctor cleaned some dirt from the wound, a coworker cleaned some brain from the rod, and in a relatively short while, Phineus and his rod were back about their business. His personality took a decided turn for the worse—and that fact is the source of his fame to this day—but the more striking thing about Phineus was just how normal he otherwise was.

For decades, mistaken medical practices and accidental damage led to research that revealed the frontal lobe's main function. The *decided turn for the worse* Phineus Gage's personality took is a polite description of what happened to him: he essentially became a *rude prick*. While he functioned normally in most ways, Phineus did not spare anyone's feelings. He would say whatever he wanted, whenever he wanted to say it, giving no thought to what might happen later. More exactly, he was rendered incapable of considering *later*, a concept which is grasped with the use of the frontal lobe.

This may seem fairly unimportant at first glance. Some people seem to hardly engage their frontal lobe at all. Nevertheless, *later* is like many concepts and abilities we take for granted. It is difficult to imagine living life with no understanding beyond right now and what has already happened. That imagining is made more difficult because if you couldn't conceive the future, you would be no better equipped to describe your idea of it than a person who is blind from birth would be able to describe what sights he wished he could see.

Without the ability to conceive the future even a few minutes ahead, it becomes very difficult to consider the consequences of words or actions; one would have to remember bad consequences from prior bad acts, the way a domesticated dog may remember his nose being rubbed in his pee when he used to go on the kitchen floor.

As gruesome as the following scenario may seem, imagine that a driver just perished in a horrific, fiery car crash. In such circumstances, a police officer is usually required to visit the victims' family, which is probably among the worst tasks an officer can be assigned. If you were in the officer's position and were met by the victim's mother, you would politely introduce yourself, ask to come inside, sit Mom down and sympathetically deliver news of the crash. Even if you had never done that before, you would likely try to be polite, speak slowly, and show compassion. A person lacking frontal lobe function could conceivably be instructed on those steps yet there is no way to prepare such a person to deal with what might follow naturally in such a scenario.

Two natural questions might come from Mom. One would be how bad the crash was. The other would be if her son suffered before he died. How would *you* answer these questions? Would you give either question a lot of thought, leaving Mom to twist in the proverbial wind as you did so? Although I don't know you, I doubt it. You would probably throw out a quick and kind answer for each, as I would too: "The scene was bad but your son passed very quickly. He didn't suffer." Even if you lack compassion, you would likely give the same answers, if only to avoid the victim's mom having a nervous breakdown on your lap. Now imagine Officer Phineus Gage in that scenario.

Mom: Was the accident a bad one?

Phineus: Jesus, what a mess! Pieces of car everywhere. Flames everywhere. And the stench? Wow! One of the worst scenes I've ever seen.

Mom: (on the verge of collapse) Oh my God! Did my boy suffer?

Phineus: Who knows? I'll tell you this, though. If he didn't die on impact, he probably suffered like a bastard.

Anyone who understands the concept of later might *think* all that our imaginary Officer Gage said above, but no one with decency would voice those thoughts. Besides, such thoughts would be relative for the first question and speculative for the second. How would you know if the victim suffered? You would hope he didn't, and you would likely leave a benign droplet or two with Mom.

One curious aspect of thought still being researched heavily is the topic of Malcolm Gladwell's *Blink: The Power of Thinking without Thinking.* What Gladwell examined wasn't the absence of thought, rather the absence of *conscious* thought. In some cases, it appears to stem from effective training such as when safe drivers unconsciously carry out the same procedures and scan for all manner of hazards each time they take the wheel, mostly without thinking about it after they become experienced.

Gladwell wrote about researchers who observed a few minutes of dialogue between spouses and predicted the future success or failure of the marriage based on established criteria. Those predictions were revealed years later to be frighteningly accurate. In other cases, it stems from exposure to certain environments which help some people predict outcomes even when they can't explain how. Two examples Gladwell provided for the latter were especially to the point. He wrote of a supposedly ancient marble statue from Greece that withstood fourteen months of investigation and scientific testing prior to the J. Paul Getty Museum in California buying it. Two foremost experts in Greek sculpture soon after viewed the sculpture and each was instantly reviled by it. They were immediately and correctly suspicious of its authenticity. It was later revealed as a fake. Although unable to immediately explain why, each took about two seconds to recognize something was amiss. Gladwell also wrote of a tennis coach who could view video taken of tennis players serving. Although the video didn't show where the ball landed, the coach could tell which serves were in and which were out. He simply couldn't explain *how* he knew.

It is entirely possible that frontal lobe function can become as seamless, effortless, and unconscious as good table manners. It may be that when someone assures a host their food will be great, consideration of the consequences of that droplet takes place but so quickly and effortlessly to be unknown to the polite guest. Arguably, then, benign droppings may be part of what makes us better as people, more human and more humane. Although those of us who sprinkle it also benefit from the lack of acrimony that can follow brutal honesty, the recipients of those droplets generally benefit too. In that sense, such droppings are benign by definition.

With BS busting, it is important to recognize what is harmless, compassionate, or beneficial. What passes the sniff test of benign droppings? I believe it is that which benefits others more than our selves and which can withstand the scrutiny of reason to come off smelling alright. Of course that's just my opinion. Based on reason, what's yours?

MALIGNANT PILES

Malignant piles are the polar opposite of benign droppings in almost every sense of the term, certainly by definition. *Malignant* is the antonym of *benign,* an adjective describing that which is very dangerous or harmful in effect. It can also describe a person who seeks to deliberately cause harm or distress. When describing a tumour, it refers to one that grows uncontrollably, invasively. As for piles, they too are the opposite of mere droppings, especially those which grow uncontrollably.

Benign droppings are used occasionally and with the best of intentions. Malignant piles are often created out of malice and show the worst aspects of BS. They are spread far and wide by some of the worst human characteristics: laziness and ignorance.

Benign droppings rarely flow from lies. A short example is the one provided in the last chapter concerning Glen's cooking. By comparison, many malignant piles start as outright lies. As they are worked into piles, however, those lies mutate because those who spread them do not necessarily know, and certainly don't care, whether the claims made by such piles are true or false, only that spreading them serves a particular purpose.

Such piles rarely stand up to reason. In fact, the very nature of them meets the definition of the fallacy *argumentum ad nauseum* (making the same claim to the point of nausea) if not several other fallacies as well. A very good example of a malignant pile was demonstrated in the United States. If you are not American, don't feel smug. Most other countries foster malignant piles too. The American media is simply so vast that they provide ample access to malignant piles.

A fierce public debate arose in the U.S. in mid 2010 concerning the plans of one Islamic group in New York City to erect a mosque in a building within blocks of the 9/11 Ground Zero site. Many people of various faiths saw this as highly inappropriate yet U.S. President Barack Obama publicly defended the rights of that group to build wherever they choose so long as they had lawful rights to the location, which this group did. Obama didn't say it was a great idea, and he acknowledged how some people may feel upset by a mosque in that location. His comments were consistent with the U.S. Constitution and current American laws, and they followed the time honoured American principle separating church and state.

Perhaps because Barack Obama's father was born and raised in Kenya, because Barack Obama was partially raised in Indonesia (a predominantly Muslim nation), because his middle name is Husain, or just because, some people came to believe he was Muslim. Eventually, some major media outlets commissioned polls to determine what percentage of Americans believed that. By early 2010, 18% of respondents believed he was a Muslim and by the summer of 2010 that rose to a whopping 24%. Most major media accompanied coverage of these polls with the clear statement that Barack Obama followed the Christian faith and always had.

Those readers unfamiliar with the *context* of this mistaken belief might wonder what the big deal was. In a country where church and state are separated by law, who cares? What separates mistaken beliefs on a large scale from malignant piles any way? In another place and time, a president's religion might mean nothing to the masses. However, the attacks of 9/11 against the U.S. were attributed to Muslim extremists, and an ongoing struggle continues between those extremists and several Western powers, chief among them the United States. Religion plays an important role in the lives of many Americans and the overwhelming majority of Americans consider themselves Christian. Even though Muslim extremists are no more representative of Islam than the Ku Klux Klan is of Christianity, many Americans, and many non-Muslim people in other western countries, remain wary of *all* Muslims. Therefore, in a country where many people distrust Muslims or their intentions, the belief that their president was Muslim posed a significant problem for a president verbally defending the rights of Muslims to build a mosque in a controversial location. In part, that's what made that mistaken belief so malignant. Furthermore, those piles flew directly in the face of documented and previously well covered facts.

Many politicians suffer publicity problems and *Candidate* Obama was no different. Perhaps the greatest of these was how publicly his Christian pastor of 20 years, Reverend Jeremiah Wright, made socially-inflammatory statements that clearly conflicted with Obama's positions. In response, Obama spoke out publicly against his pastor, who soon after became his *former* pastor. Nevertheless, Reverend Wright's ranting was referred to many times by Americans opposed to Obama becoming their president. This begs an important question: Did those opposed to Obama from the beginning forget their earlier dislike of him based on the ranting of his long-time pastor? I suspect not. They avoided any reasoned thought whatsoever.

Nothing spreads malignant piles better or faster than a vacuum of thought.

Most politicians and pundits are well educated, no matter what part of the political spectrum they occupy. Since millions of people within and outside the U.S. already knew Barack Obama was Christian, and millions more could pick that up from the web in mere seconds, you can be sure his public critics knew the truth too. Nevertheless, they were conspicuously absent on this Muslim issue. Why? Perhaps because it served their purpose for millions of Americans to believe something perceived as negative about their political opponent.

Whoever started that rumour may very well have known better, which would make the root of that pile a lie. If it wasn't an outright lie, though, it nevertheless revealed an absence of thought that resulted in a mistaken belief among virtually one quarter of Americans polled on the issue. If those polls were accurate, roughly 75 million Americans swallowed that pungent pile.

Why so many words to address one pile? Because the most effective cure for such piles are facts, which often require words. The more facts, the more words are required to express and explain those. The people who most often shovel malignant piles like to keep things *short and sweet.*

I address issue of the not-Muslim-president to illustrate several aspects of malignant piles, none which are stopped by national borders or language barriers. Misinformation can spread like wild fire if one group has an interest in it spreading, no matter how untrue it is, and no matter how easily enquiring minds can discover that. Regardless of how stupid or ludicrous a particular pile is, it can spread virally if enough people choose to switch their critical minds off. The more people spreading the pile, the less popular it becomes to point at it and hold your nose. For these reasons alone, anyone who thinks for himself should step away from malignant piles, thus seeing them for the pungent crap they are. There's at least one more reason you should avoid pungent piles but that takes a bit of background.

History is filled with all sorts of terrible acts based upon malignant piles. World-wide wars have resulted from such piles, as have several genocides, persecutions, botched medical procedures, and other really bad acts. None of those bad acts stemmed from benign droppings. Messed-up beliefs flourished from piles that kept spreading and spreading with no reasonable challenge in sight. The wider these beliefs were accepted the more dire consequences which greeted anyone who challenged them.

The Spanish Inquisition was carried out by a branch of the Roman Catholic Church against anyone who challenged the precise beliefs voiced by that church's leadership at that time. Challenging the wisdom or rightness of those beliefs could put people under the tortuous eye of the Inquisition's guardians, even if they challenged no other aspect of that religion. Nazi Germany was no more welcoming a place for anyone who questioned the accuracy and wisdom of Hitler's regime, whether that was going to war against any nation in its way or shipping off Jews to, well, very few Germans seemed to know or ask. Labour and death camps, as it turned out. Malignant piles were also behind mistaken beliefs widely held by the majority within given regions of the globe for many centuries, from the earth being flat to monarchs being chosen by God. For all I know, several beliefs I hold, and maybe some of yours, may be based on malignant piles.

Some people like to describe beliefs and opposing people as *questionable*. In truth, almost every belief and person is questionable. Nothing and no one should be considered so perfect and so right as to be beyond logical questions. Like reasonable people, reasonable ideas stand up very well to challenges based on reason. Most reasonable people actually welcome questions to promote discussion, and to know for themselves if their ideas hold up. "It stands to reason" is a common expression describing ideas which do just that.

Ultimately, the more we are willing to accept that our beliefs are possibly flawed, the less likely those beliefs will be piles and the less effectively piles will spread *to* us or onward *from* us. There is just one catch: human nature can get in the way of open minds and challenges from other people. One of the strongest aspects of that nature is ego.

I don't like the idea of being wrong or misled. You probably don't either. Yet I know I'm not perfect. As one of my former college instructors liked to say, "The Romans crucified the last guy who was perfect." Since I'm not perfect and likely a lot farther from perfection than I realize, it's quite possible I'm wrong about some beliefs I hold. Such a realization requires that I keep my ears and eyes open for information that conflicts with my beliefs, and that I examine information with critical reason, out of habit and with as little effort as habits require. Accordingly, I base my acceptance of information on how well or not it holds up to a sniff test.

Some people and groups can undermine that kind of examination, hence providing excellent breeding grounds for infectious poop piles. First, few people *like* to think of themselves as being wrong. Second, groups of people such as voters gravitate toward candidates who seem the most confident in their statements. When a politician changes his or her stated position on a given issue that person is often said to have *flip flopped*, which is usually seen as weakness. Some people certainly change positions for less than seemly reasons such as secret deals or exchanges of support for other issues, or even bribery in one form or another. Yet other reasons for changing a belief include new information, and new examination of old information.

Imagine being elected as mayor of a major city. Let's say you campaigned to eliminate a particular program to save taxpayer's money but then saw the value of that program once you got a closer look at the program due to being mayor. What would you do then? Would you follow through on what you later learned was a bad idea, or would you change your mind and explain why? In that moment, you might face a choice between *keeping* your job past the next election and *doing* your job now. That partially explains why some politicians and others *stick to their guns* even when facts make doing so less reasonable. This also explains why some people *do* change their minds.

It's safe to say *some* Americans have a strong dislike for Muslim's (as do *some* people in other countries too). I believe that particular dislike stems from fear or distrust, largely based on the coordinated terror attacks best known by the date they were carried out, 9/11 (of 2001). That's understandable, and unfortunate. Those attacks were carried out by a small number of extremist Muslims. As with Christians, Jews, Sikhs and many other faiths, Muslims share some common beliefs, yet the details of those beliefs separate them into differing groups within their larger faith. Just as there are various *denominations* of Christianity (Catholic and *Protestant* ones such as Presbyterian and Baptist) and differing sects of other faiths, there are differing sects of Islam. Just as Catholics and some Protestant groups have violently clashed in some regions, even in recent decades in Northern Ireland, differing sects within Islam have also clashed, sometimes violently. Just as the most extremist Christians are often feared and reviled by other Christians, Muslim *jihadists* are the most violent among Islam, feared and reviled within many of that faith. Accordingly, those who fear or distrust *all* Muslims could better serve their cause, whether safety or revenge, by focusing their negative emotions on those Muslim groups that follow the same slant on Islam the jihadists do. Just as being a Christian doesn't mean white hoods and burning crosses, being Muslim doesn't make someone a jihadist or sympathetic to them. If only for efficiency, then, wouldn't it make sense to focus on the *real* bad guys?

Muslim extremists also target Muslims who they believe betray Islam. Such jihadists often issue public pronouncements of war and death against Muslim individuals and groups they don't like. Among those *condemned to death* groups is an Islamic sect known as *Sufi,* whose followers use colourful costumes and music as part of their ceremonies. Muslim extremists see such practices as degenerate.

Here is the irony of this malignant pile: The Mulsims who drew so much hostility over the proposed mosque in lower Manhattan are Sufis. They fear Muslim terrorism as much as anyone else. The more Sufis there are and the more attention they get, the more pissed off Muslim extremists might be. You would think Americans opposed to radical Islam would take every opportunity to poke a stick in their enemies' eye they could. Instead, large numbers directed their dislike towards the whole faith of Islam, all one billion of them. Instead of asking why a guy as well-educated and well-informed as the United States' President backed a Muslim group's rights, large numbers were sucked into a malignant pile that suggested something sinister or self-serving in his opinions. In the process, a golden opportunity to symbolically stick it to radical Islamists was lost by the very people most inclined to do just that.

That's what makes malignant piles so dangerously pungent. Such piles not only harm those they are meant to. Quite often, those piles also hurt those who do the spreading. Many other examples on the small and large scale exist, historically and currently, and many of them are far worse than missed opportunities.

Screenwriter Aaron Sorkin, creator and writer of such films as *A Few Good Men* and television series as *The West Wing,* touched on this aspect of malignant piles. In *An American President,* Sorkin's title character addressed the press corps about a senator who repeatedly slammed him with malignant piles while preparing to run against him in the next election. Part way through his impromptu address, he touched on that aspect,

> I've known Bob Rumsden for years and I've been operating on the assumption that the reason he spends so much time screaming at the rain is that he simply doesn't get it. Well, I was wrong. Bob's problem isn't that he doesn't *get it.* Bob's problem is that *he can't sell it.*
>
> We have serious problems to solve and we need serious people to solve them. But whatever you particular problem is, I promise you, Bob Rusmden is not the least bit interested in solving it. He is interested in two thing and two things only: Making you *afraid* of it and telling you who's to *blame* for it. *That,* ladies and gentlemen, is how you win elections.

History shows with abundant examples just how accurate Sorkin is on this point, as well as how poorly events often turn out for the very people who swallow and spit out malignant piles. When Germany suffered financial collapse and political upheaval following the First World War, Adolf Hitler blamed communists and Jews for Germany's problems. Over time, more and more German's accepted his piles until Hitler ran Germany. Within a few years of reaching power, Hitler persecuted Germany's Jews and then conquered most of Europe, and had Jews throughout those countries hunted down too. Millions of Jews and others were killed in death camps due to Hitler's malignant piles yet millions of Germans were killed or injured in battlefields and bombings through that country being flattened, as much as many nations she previously invaded. So much for ignorance being bliss.

Germans aren't the only people who previously swallowed pile upon pile. So too did some Turks during the Armenian genocide and some Cambodians during their genocide. Later still, Uganda's Idi Amin blamed his country's problems on the educated, business-oriented Ugandans of Indian descent, driving them out. Things only got worse for the *real* Ugandans after that.

Look at the tide of gang and drug violence in North America so well publicized in recent years. Advocates for some urban groups blame the government and the *system* for gangs being so strong and people in affected neighbourhoods enabling them. Yet no matter how much money is spent on new programs and inquiries, the problems persist or even grow. Like so many other social problems, that phenomenon crosses racial and geographic barriers, mostly because BS does too.

Malignant piles are easy to stop in the early stages, very difficult to stop in later ones. Stoppable they are, though. Everyone on either side of an issue has a stake in stopping them. Locally and internationally, history shows that malignant piles often hurt those who the piles are about *as well as* those who do the swallowing and spreading.

When someone does something truly stupid, it's very common for someone else to ask, "What was he *thinking*?" When large groups demonstrate equal stupidity, the question is the same, "What were *they* thinking?" Isn't it obvious? They *weren't* thinking, not truly. Isn't the answer to how you and I can stop malignant piles equally obvious?

IGNORANCE

I n the previous chapter I discussed malignant piles, how they spread as well as why some people swallow and spread them. That might suggest that those who accept and multiply BS are stupid or less intelligent than others. Not at all. What renders some people more susceptible to BS than others is not stupidity, it is ignorance. Like BS, ignorance is often misunderstood so understanding it helps us to overcome it and be far less susceptible to stinky piles of any kind.

Some people believe *ignorant* is synonymous with *rude*. Many more believe that to be ignorant is to be stupid, yet very little connects the two. *Ignorant* is defined as lacking in knowledge or training, unlearned, uninformed on a particular subject or generally. That might seem the same as stupid, intellectually deficient, or cognitively challenged but it is not necessarily any of those. As we see shortly, a formal education is no guarantee against ignorance, and many people who lack formal education are able-bodied BS busters.

Physician, philosopher, and philanthropist Albert Schweitzer was said, "The problem with man today is that he simply doesn't *think*." Bearing in mind that Dr. Schweitzer died in 1965, lack of thought is hardly a new issue. I don't believe he meant that humans are *unable* to think, rather that large numbers do not *bother* to think.

Ignorance is not the inability to know or gain knowledge. It is the lack of knowledge coupled with the lack of any interest in gaining knowledge. Put another way, ignorant people do not *know* and do not *care* to know. Therefore, a lack of intellectual potential is not what makes one ignorant; a lack of intellectual *interest* is.

When I discussed reasoning I pointed out that it is rarely taught in an explicit way within formal educational programs, at least in recent times. Reasoning is required in many courses of study and, therefore, it is *implicitly* taught. However, if either the student or instructor fails to make such connections, the implicit lessons simply do not happen. In essence, many formal academic programs approach reasoning the same way a blind man might approach tennis.

On the other end of the academic scale, many people implicitly learn to reason through day-to-day conversation with friends, mentors, coaches, and family members. One of the most effective places where reasoning is learned is at the family dinner table when a variety of topics are casually discussed. Sadly, the family dinner is becoming less and less common in many households, whether rich or poor, black, white or any other skin colour. Nevertheless, the mere fact that reasoning can be implicitly learned outside of the classroom means the skill is attainable by people of all walks of life, even without formal education.

Many people are unaware of their abilities to reason even though they demonstrate those on a daily basis. People often refer to this as *common sense*, which is none too common. If something makes *sense*, it is reasonable and people of all backgrounds can understand it whether their backgrounds are common or not. All they need is an interest in finding truth and accuracy in whatever they discuss. Those discussions can be what renovations will increase your home's value, what kind of car someone should buy to meet her needs, or why so-and-so's daughter shouldn't date the village idiot.

You can find people every day who speak accurately and truly about whatever they discuss. You can work on being one of those people too, if you aren't already. The more you do it, the more it becomes a habit, and the more BS will catch your well-tuned ear and reasonable mind.

I referred in the last chapter to terrible things sometimes done by large groups of people. If there is a hierarchy to bad acts, genocide must surely be at the top of anyone's list. Some readers may presume that those who commit genocide are uneducated folks doing what some evil leader told them to. Sometimes that has been the case but other times not. In 1970s Cambodia, the ruling regime wanted to reform the country into a simple agricultural state, so its leaders saw educated people such as doctors, lawyers, teachers, and writers as a threat, and did its utmost to kill them, all of them. That genocide saw about a third of the population murdered. In Cambodia then, a lack of education may certainly have led people to swallowing what was shovelled. Let's look at another example, though.

I do not believe any nationality or race is genetically predisposed to great intelligence or a lack thereof. Still I believe cultural trends play a significant role in some nations being stronger than others in some fields, if only through collective interest and focused work. For instance, present day India and China are each renowned for cranking out millions of well-educated, highly-skilled people able to perform highly-technical work. Germany was and still is renowned for its technical prowess and culture of efficiency, even when that country's people accepted train loads of malignant piles. Many major technical advances started during the Nazi regime. They were the first nation to develop jet aircraft and might have ruled the skies to win the Second World War if they had got them into regular production a year or two sooner than they did. They were also the first nation to work on nuclear weapons. The reason the United States put a huge, secret program together partway through that war to develop the atomic bomb was to do so *before* Germany did. What made that scenario even scarier was that German scientists had already developed rockets and used them to deliver large bombs on England. Decades ago, "What are you, a *rocket scientist*?" was commonly-used challenge in North America to mock someone who appeared to be too smart. In Nazi Germany, an astonishing number of people could have truthfully answered, "*Ja! Ich bin*"(Yes, I am), or "*Nein, aber mein Vater ist*" (No, but my father is). The race between the U.S. and former Soviet Union many years later, into space and to the moon, was largely a race between the Germans who America recruited after Nazi Germany collapsed and the Germans captured or recruited by the Soviets. When the U.S. reached the moon first in 1969 some American leaders joked, "*Our Germans were better than theirs.*"

My point is to illustrate this: massive gobs of intelligence and education did not stop at least some of these geniuses in Nazi Germany from blindly following BS of the highest order. Ample evidence of this was uncovered at Peenemunde, home to the German rocket program. Evidence shows that as many as 20,000 slave labourers from concentration camps were used to build the weapons deep underground, where they would not be seen by Allied air reconnaissance. The founder of the German missile program was Wernher Von Braun, later the technical leader of the early U.S. space program. Tony Paterson of the British newspaper *The Telegraph* wrote of this in his 2001 story, *Germans at last learn truth about von Braun's 'space research' base*: In the story, "A Polish slave-labour survivor of the Dora factory recalled how Wernher von Braun visited the works and seemed 'completely unperturbed' by the piles of corpses."

By all accounts for or against Von Braun, he was a highly-intelligent, vastly-educated man. So how could he show no more concern for piles of corpses and slave labourers than un-educated soldiers did later in Cambodia, and uneducated tribesman did later in Rwanda? If he chose to, surely Von Braun could have seen how unreasonable, evil, and inhumane Nazi policies and practices were. It seems to me, then, that he and a host of other well-educated Germans did precisely what Dr. Albert Schweitzer later referred to. They simply did not *think*, not in all the ways that mattered.

Those of the glass-is-half-empty mindset may take this as depressing, that even geniuses at the top of their game can be hoodwinked by silver-tongued BSers. Well, I can crap my pants if I don't bother to stroll to the nearest bathroom when the need arises, yet choose I go to a bathroom instead. It isn't even a conscious choice for you or I since the pants-crapping option doesn't occur to us after we establish better habits as young children. Therefore, I argue that susceptibility to BS is not borne of deficient intellect rather deficient *application* of intellect.

As luck would have it, I grew up with many children whose parents grew up in Nazi Germany. A few of my friends' fathers fought in the German army in the Second World War. My own father suffered as a young child in Nazi occupied Holland. My mother's young life was turned upside down as her family was moved to a Royal Air Force base where battered, one-winged planes sometimes returned from missions over Germany, and there was a constant threat of German air strikes. One of my former bosses is the son of one of Von Braun's assistants, one who was captured by the Soviets and never seen by his family again. Perhaps because of my friendships from early on, I don't condemn Germans, Cambodians,

Rwandans, Turks, or any other group just because *some* of their countrymen did really bad things. In each of those places and many more, reasonable people stood up to stupid ideas or undermined them through secret means. For instance, the German underground movement tried to assassinate Hitler, snuck Jews and other targeted people out of Germany, and gathered military intelligence for Allied spies. In crime-ridden neighbourhoods today, reasonable citizens speak out against gangs, or they quietly feed information to police so those who destroy their communities can be sent packing, preferably to jail.

Each identifiable group associated with really bad acts has those in their midst who saw reason and tried to do the right thing. It wasn't always easy or even safe, but it was possible and the most-reasonable course of action, then and now. As Edmund Burke once wrote, "All that is required for the triumph of evil is that good men do nothing."

Not every thoughtless act is evil, but thoughtless states of mind certainly provide fertile ground for BS, some which leads to stupid acts or millions of them. Ignorance is the key to malignant BS. Hence, recognizing, pointing out, challenging, and eradicating ignorance are the keys to fighting malignant BS. That it can also be fun to bust BS is merely a bonus.

INDICATORS

As you may recall from the Reasoning chapter, an inference indicator is a word or punctuation mark implicitly indicating that what follows it is connected to what was just provided. For instance: "My wife hit me in the forearm with a frying pan and now it's bent at a pretty-gross angle. *So* I think it's broken." Like many aspects of reasoning, the use of inference indicators is often a conscious act, at least until reasoning becomes a well-established habit. Not all indicators are so useful, and not all indicators are revealed on purpose.

Someone with a bad case of gas, for instance, may unconsciously or unavoidably release some of it around other people, thus indicating to everyone around him that he has gas, if not also a bad diet. A similar kind of indicator appears frequently in poker. When some players bluff or have a very good hand, they make slight gestures or expressions indicating one way or the other. It is completely self-defeating to indicate what kind of hand you have, yet a number of poker players unwittingly do just that. An experienced poker player can spot those indicators in an opponent if he has seen the opponent's pattern of behaviour. Such an indicator is known in poker as a *tell*.

The world of poop speak also has its share of tells, some verbal, others physical. For obvious reasons, I like to call these *BS Indicators*. Like tells, they are virtually always unconscious. Those who BS others don't want to be called on that. In particular, malignant piles involve a lack of mental effort so it is not surprising that poop speakers so often reveal their poop, albeit accidentally. In essence, these indicators tell the trained or observant individual that what is about to follow is quite possibly crap.

There are four kinds of rules humans deal with, one which is the general rule. As a general rule jumping off a cliff is a very bad idea. General rules are not created rules such as criminal laws, and they do not flow from unwavering natural laws such as gravity. In the strictest sense, they are not rules at all. They are merely observable facts which usually apply. When you see *this* it usually means *that*. Because they are not specific, general rules have exceptions. For instance, jumping off a cliff at a Sandals resort may not be a bad idea at all, especially if it is designated for that purpose and it overhangs deep water.

BS indicators work in much the same way. As a general rule, when someone says or gives a BS indicator, poop usually follows. While *tells* in poker are different for each player, BS indicators seem fairly similar among most people, at least those who speak English. Like general rules, no BS indicator is an ironclad guarantee that what follows will stink, and some of these indicators apply to outright lies too. There are no specified lists to go by but I do my best to start one here. The examples I provide are but a few of the many I have seen or heard through my years. Some of them will seem familiar to most readers, hopefully from hearing them more than spewing them out.

Naturally, it is possible that you toss out one of more of the indicators I provide below, or a host of others I don't. I'm sure I have tossed out a fair number too. It is also possible that you have been a bit of a BSer yourself. Again, same here. If so, it's not the end of the world for either of us. It is merely a heads up to think a little more. That's all. Think a little more than you might currently in some circumstances.

You can be sure that since I have figured these indicators out, many other people have too. Whether or not other people have labels for what they hear doesn't really matter. If one or more of these indicators currently applies to you, *currently* is the operative word to work on.

Since there is no set list of BS indicators, there is no limit to the number of indicators you can observe and file away for future reference. I provide a few common examples for you to start your own catalogue with:

"Just": While sentences can very from *I was just* to *It's just that* to *I just*, that central word is the give away. I provided an example of this indicator starting in the third paragraph of the Preface. A guy was parked illegally in a shopping plaza when I confronted him about that. No doubt because I was standing next to a uniformed cop at the time, the lazy driver hit the poop button, "I'm just waiting for my wife. She's just in the drug store." I've seen other drivers rush out to cars parked illegally, telling the cop or parking control officer "I was just a minute," even if he was in the mall for an hour. Either driver could easily say, "I was being lazy" or "I know I shouldn't park here, sorry." Yet the stink flows out preceded by an indicator of that.

A teenaged daughter saunters through the front door at 2 A.M. looking like the mess she is at that time. Her worried mom or dad asks why she wasn't home at 11 P.M. as she promised before going out. "I was *just* with a few friends," she blurts out defensively, "I wasn't doing anything." Aside from being non-responsive, this girl has just told her parents a lot more than she meant to. From hearing only those few words, they can't know what she *was* doing, but they can bet it wasn't anything they will be pleased about if or when they find out.

If you think I'm off base here, listen the next time you hear *just*. There is, however, a common exception to this general rule, when it concerns something occurring recently. An example: *I was just on the phone with Mary, who said she's running late.* Another example would be *I just arrived and don't know if my husband is here yet.*

"I don't know": This seems a fairly straightforward, harmless sentence and it *can* be true. After all, no one knows everything, so it seems a reasonable response every now and then. Still, the quicker it comes out, the greater the chance that what follows will smell. If someone considers the question before saying he doesn't know, it is far more likely he gave the question some thought and came up empty. As we have seen from several angles already, BS and conscious thought are usually incompatible. That's why this indicator so commonly used. It's not that BSers don't *know* as much as they don't *care*.

"I swear to _____": Although the usual words are *I swear to God*, other variations include *I swear on my mother* or other treasured relatives, usually female. Grandmothers are a favoured choice. Unlike most indicators that pop out just before the crap, this one usually comes right after the crap and a short pause, during which the crap sender notices looks of disbelief on the listener's face. Those who speak the truth usually don't care whether everyone believes them; truth tellers know they are telling the truth, which favours them if or when it is revealed. BSers often have a stake in their poop being accepted, or feel they do, so they grow desperate when they suspect people are not buying what they are selling. As for what might be revealed in the future, poop speakers don't think about that at the time. Incidentally, this indicator often applies to lies as well.

Absolutes: There are times when an absolute declaration is truthful, usually in the negative, such as when a vegetarian says she never eats meat or when a non-smoker says he never smokes. In the majority of cases, however, absolutes serve as an excellent stink indicator. Imagine you saw a grocery store cashier arguing with a customer who claimed to have received incorrect change, "I always give correct change, so there's no way I short changed you." This would be in stark contrast to the cashier recalling specifics, such as when the customer went through her check-out twenty minutes ago with her little girl, what bills she paid with, that sort of thing. Another version of this indicator comes up concerning driving, when someone says he never speeds. A far more credible claim would be to say "I try never to speed, I watch my speedometer like a hawk, and I usually drive in the slow lane so faster drivers don't go right up my rear bumper."

What absolutes usually do, not always because *that* would be an absolute, is to avoid specific recollections by tossing out claims of perfection. Beware anyone who implies he is perfect. Also, wonder why he isn't addressing the specific issue you are talking about, if only to say he's unsure or can't remember the specifics but *usually* does this or that.

"Everyone" and "Everybody": This indicator is a favourite among people who routinely make bad choices. It is also used by people who want to convince others that they are out of touch, isolated in their belief or non-belief. The girl who smokes weed every other day says, "Everybody's doing it." The steroid monkey in the gym says, "Everyone who is a serious athlete does this stuff."

The racist idiot in school says, "Everyone knows you can't trust (pick a racial group)."

For starters, these statements are claims without any logic behind them. Even if they act as premises for a larger argument, such arguments are fallacious (argument to numbers or *argumentum ad numerum*). Moreover, these claims are so easy to shoot down with one simple rebuttal: *You're* part of everyone and if you aren't doing it, obviously everyone *isn't*. If there is at least one exception to an absolute claim, there are likely dozens, hundreds, or millions more.

Never Wrong: As discussed in prior pages, those who seek the truth in any matter are open to being corrected, no matter how inconvenient that may be in a given situation. Who among us is perfect? From time to time, any of us is wrong about *something*. Accordingly, this indicator is also a variation of an absolute.

This particular indicator rarely comes up once. More often, it is a cumulative indicator about the person who spews poop and/or lies. Some people feel the need to be right all the time in every situation no matter what. The root of that personality trait is beyond my expertise but I know people with it exist because I had the mixed fortune to work with two of them.

Such people seem far less concerned with being right than being *accepted* as right. Since the truth may be something other than what a certain person believes, if that person appears determined all the time to be accepted as right, that's a fairly logical indicator that truth and accuracy are secondary to ego for him or her. In fairness to the fairer gender, both the people I've known with this trait are men, both turned out to be regular if not pathological liars. I learned about one of them lying after he was arrested (and later jailed) following a detailed investigation.

Attacker Mode: As discussed previously, everything is *questionable* to some degree. That which is presented as beyond question may not stand up to questions very well. People are the same. Those who take a scientific approach to information naturally question at least some of what they hear and see. In that questioning, some things will stick and others will be tossed away as poop of one sort or another. By comparison, those who take a propagandist's approach want to win the contest whether a verbal dispute or something larger. Winning with what he says is more important to a propagandist than anything else.

Those familiar with many sports or with chess know the value of being offensive in nature. As an old saying goes, *the best defence is a good offence.* Many animals of lesser intellectual capacity than your average human instinctively adopt this approach in the face of whatever they perceive as danger. Think of a cornered stray cat or a mother bear whose cubs wander into an occupied camp ground and you get the idea. The need to win overcomes some people who habitually shovel poop. When previous attempts to defend their piles fail, or when they can't come up with a credible defence for their positions, some of these people strike out with remarkable ferocity. Fortunately, that attack is usually verbal. This can include all sorts of personal attacks, attacks on an irrelevant topic, shouting down an opposing view or an opposing person. Such displays are not thought out. Instead they appear to be instinctive, driven, angry, or even desperate.

This kind of attack can be seen in bars, basements, and backyards all over the globe but so too can it be seen on television news shows when one or more participants disagree with others with opposing views. The debates between the leaders of federal parties in many countries can descend into shouting matches showing all the tact and manners of hungry dogs at a small chow bowl. Sadly, I have seen that myself in my own country.

Non-answers: While this is a variation of a few previously cited indicators and is often fallacious (*arguing off point* or *straw man*, for examples), these are often indicators of something fishy. Think back to our imaginary cashier speaking in absolutes about always giving correct change to customers. Saying she always gives correct change would not address whether or not she did in one specific instance. It would be a non-answer.

Parliament and other political venues provide many examples of non-answers without picking on imaginary grocery-store cashiers. I remember one particular exchange during which the leader of the Official Opposition asked the Prime Minister of the day (not the current one) if he previously met a certain gentleman for lunch, as was being reported in the news. This other gentleman was in the midst of a bribery scandal involving the Prime Minister's party, so the question was highly relevant. The Prime Minister responded by accusing the Opposition party of trying to dismantle health care programs. My reaction was to accidentally utter a Scooby-Doo-like "Huh?" I wish the Opposition leader had followed with this question: "Could the Prime Minister please tell the House, was that a *Yes* or a *No*?" He didn't.

Rumours: We are all familiar with rumours. Most of us know at least a few people who love to repeat them as often as possible. That rumours are potentially harmful is well known. That rumours can be BS is not so well known because the nature of the latter is so rarely discussed.

As most people know, some rumours turn out to be true whether they concern "inappropriate" relations between a former US President and an intern or someone getting a good grade due to similar favours. As people also know, many rumours result from true information being morphed into untruths through frequent and erroneous telling, or from being untrue from the start.

As much as I despise the *gotcha* style of some journalists, at least that profession generally observes a noble rule. Most principled journalists do not report rumours they have not been able to confirm with least three independent sources. While some journalists will drop that standard to one source, that at least shows a degree of principle, attaching the information to a person instead of the ubiquitous, nameless *they.*

The most ambitious rumour mongers among us don't bother putting a source to rumours. They merely repeat rumours in a way that makes the information no more accurate than the end result of broken telephone. In that way, rumours meet the definition of BS more than most types of information. How can you consider the source if you haven't the foggiest idea who that is?

Pretence: Years ago, I was speaking with a guy I grew up with. As part of his university program, he worked in an African relief project for the better part of a year. While away on this mission, he later told me, things suddenly became *incredibly, amazingly, unbelievably, absolutely unambiguous* for him. You or I might have said things became *clear.* If either of us were especially impassioned about things, we might say they became *really clear* or *very clear.* This wouldn't be because the longer words were intimidating to us. A dictionary could demystify those words in any case. It would be because we were speaking plainly, openly, engaging in *straight talk.* Straight talk is a term often associated with truth. When someone dresses up a description for little useful purpose, his actions can often be described as *pretentious* whether or not that dressing applies to language.

I have no doubt things became clear for my former friend. However, the pretentious (and redundant) way he expressed it immediately set off my poop meter, long before I even knew one of those existed. As time and experience later showed, that guy became increasingly enamoured of excrement like notions. Sorry, I mean he bought into more and more crap. Sure, the crap he spat out was far more groomed and better presented than what he originally swallowed but I suspect that sugar-covered manure is better presented than the straight variety too, yet it is still manure.

Pretence can also take the form of non-answers. One of my favourite examples, quite favoured by pretentious people, is the term *per se*, an adverb that means intrinsically, within itself, and/or innately. Imagine that a friend of yours just grabbed a shoplifter exiting a store and I asked you if she was a police officer, and you answered, "Not per se, but she works at the store", that would be an accurate use of the term. This temporary crime fighter would be performing a function usually done by police, or people employed or contracted by the store to catch thieves within specific business locations. By contrast, when I hear the term used, it is usually in the response to a direct question, such as "Did you tell your doctor about your massive headaches and dizzy spells?" A *not-per-se* response there would not answer the question one way or the other. I have even heard that answer in response to whether or not a particular male is the father of a yet-to-arrive baby.

By definition, *pretence* is a false show of something, the act of pretending or something otherwise false, as in obtaining money under false pretences. I don't have a problem with using language effectively or expanding my vocabulary but I know from experience just how good an indicator of stink pretentious words can be.

Impossibilities: These are yet another variation of absolutes, albeit with a twist. Whereas most people who use absolutes try to defend their own beliefs or claims, those who use impossibilities are most often trying to defend someone else. Looking back on O.J. Simpson's criminal trial and putting the ugly race stuff aside, there was a persistent claim by Simpson supporters that he could not have possibly committed that terrible crime because he was such a great football player in his time. If Simpson were playing football at the time the victims were killed, *that* would be relevant. Otherwise, it wasn't.

Impossibilities are claimed on behalf of celebrities, relatives, and others. "He just couldn't have done it. He's not that kind of guy." Serial killers, in particular, love that kind of blanket denial on the part of relatives or neighbours. As for parental denials, the Jamaican's have a great saying for when a mother or father claims it is impossible their son performed a bad misdeed: *A fisherman never says his fish stink.*

I have seen many instances when a student was believed by staff to have done something wrong, perhaps taking a classmate's property or assaulting someone. On many occasions, I have seen parents show up or a principal step up on the youth's behalf, strongly denying the youth is guilty of whatever the student is accused of. Interestingly and in most cases, no one had yet told the parents or principal what the youth was suspected of. It was as if these parents and administrators were saying, "I don't know what you think this boy did, but it's impossible he did anything bad, *whatever* it is." Without the first clue what the possibilities are, that is a hollow claim and BS, even if the person in question is innocent. Supporting your children or students is a good instinct, but it is important to let a few facts and thought enter the mix too or else a wayward youth can become a more wayward youth and then a wayward adult. Furthermore, most wayward people do not de-escalate their bad acts without serious intervention of some kind.

Absence of Options: This indicator differs entirely from impossibilities, although it sounds similar. It is favoured by people who continually, chronically make bad decisions and then claim there were no other courses of action available than what they took.

Street-gang members and those who follow their behaviour patterns are excellent examples. The proof of my argument was amply provided by an underground video entitled *The Real Toronto*. It showed gang members and assorted thugs from several crime-ridden areas in that city. This wasn't a documentary, rather a collection of segments, each where an unseen videographer recorded various self-proclaimed thugs addressing the camera. They talked about what they do and what gangs or gang affiliations they represent. In some instances, they showed off the guns they carry. One fired a sawed off shotgun into the air behind a high-rise apartment building. There was no questioning of these guys, merely a platform for them to say whatever they wanted.

It was a tough video to watch because it was so mind-numbing. The language used was so strewn with profanity to be at once vague and boring, offering little social benefit and no entertainment value. Most of all, it was tough to watch because it was so *repetitive*. Although the neighbourhoods, ages, and racial backgrounds differed, the same logical void was spewed by most subjects on screen, particularly their claim that they live the way they do because of *where* they live.

"I live in the hood so I gotta hussle." *Hussle* is the universal term these guys used to describe anything from extortion to robbery to drug peddling to prostitution. Never mind that many success stories spring from the very same neighbourhoods and conditions that spawned these criminals. Never mind that they have the same access to resources and education others in those same neighbourhoods avail themselves of. Never mind that no racial or geographic group has ever been shown to have criminals as the majority of their number. If these guys applied reasoned thought to their situations, if they developed that skill, they would have seen options. In the same way poop speak so often works, these guys didn't bother. They took the only course of action they *bothered* to see and spent a lot of time trying to convince others such as family members, friends, and advocates that no other options existed. Strangely, many relatives, friends, and advocates seem to swallow these piles even though they came from the same circumstances but created far more functional lives.

A similar indicator is tossed out with equal abandon by terrorists of every stripe, colour, and religion. The excuse is always the same: they have no other choice or option.

While it may seem extreme to liken urban street thugs to terrorists, take a closer look at their claim of no options, as well as the cumulative effect on the very people and areas they claim to support. Then draw your own conclusions.

Repetition: While unrelated to other indicators and a fallacy by definition (argumentum ad nauseum), it is also an excellent poop indicator. Unfortunately, spotting it is a bit tricky. It requires considerable understanding of reason to sort the poop from the truth when this speech device is used.

Many honest, well-meaning people use repetition to make good things happen. Positive self-talk and constructive cheerleading by other people are two benign examples. When an athlete tells himself he can win the next game, it may not be based on cold reason. It *has* helped many people succeed where others thought they would fail, even where all the observable facts in the world indicated they would fail. "You can do it." is a common cheer supporters will say to help someone erase self-doubt that can be self-defeating. These are harmless, benign droppings.

Politicians, business people, military leaders, and others often use another kind of repetition, which political commentators refer to as *staying on message*. Repetition is used by such people in the realization that, quite often, messages will not stick without repetition. On the other side of the repetition coin is the malignant type. Adolf Hilter's chief of propaganda, Joseph Goebbels, was quoted thusly: "If you tell a lie big enough and keep repeating it, people will eventually come to believe it." So how can one tell the difference between benign repetition and the more-sinister variety? Goebbels went on to say,

> The lie can be maintained only for such time as the State can shield the people from the political, economic and/or military consequences of the lie. It thus becomes vitally important for the State to use all of its powers to repress dissent, for the truth is the mortal enemy of the lie, and thus by extension, the truth is the greatest enemy of the State.

By Goebbels' explanation, and few people in history are more recognized as poo peddlers than he, *dissent* and *truth* are the enemies of propaganda. Hence, they are also the enemy of malignant, potentially harmful BS. That which can withstand dissent, that which does not conflict with the truth, is far less likely to be BS than that which avoids it. Of course, this applies to people as well.

The list of potential BS indicators can go on and on but I won't. Some indicators can be physical too. You can collect and catalogue your own list in the same way for physical cues as for verbal ones. Of note is how some of these verbal and physical indicators can also reveal lies. In each case, liars reveal themselves just as unconsciously as poop speakers do.

On a cautionary note, do not assume BS or a lie is coming in *every* instance of every indicator. There are exceptions to most situations and *all* general rules; BS indicators are general rules. Also, poop speakers and liars often show more than one indicator in a given case of shovelling. By contrast, an honest person can make a verbal or reasoning error here and there while still trying to find true information, or pass on true information. Thinking back to the Reasoning chapter, consider how much more probable a conclusion is when more premises support it. The more BS indicators someone unwittingly throws out, the more probable it is that the person is BSing.

No single tool can be used for every task but a steadily growing collection of tools can increase one's success at any task, in this case BS busting.

REVELATIONS

As biblical as this chapter title sounds, you probably know the word as merely the result of something being revealed. Indicators are handy to the trained ear for detecting pungent piles when they are first spewed out. Another aspect of BS is often detectable to trained *eyes*. Some noticeable actions reveal a strong *susceptibility* to a whole range of piles. In simple terms, some people's words and actions serve as revelations of BS. In other cases, the words or actions of these people are so thoughtless as to suggest that if they harbour any beliefs at all, those are rife with crap of all kinds.

Poop revelations are all around us and easy to spot. As with indicators, you can compile your own list with time and minimal mental effort. While they are similar to indicators, they differ in one notable way. Revelations are observable in many people's day-to-day actions, yet not every action of the same type serves as a revelation.

Too cryptic? Consider the act of driving a motor vehicle, something many adults in the world do. Driving does not reveal BS yet how *some* people drive reveals a lot about their lack of thought, which makes them highly susceptible to BS. As with indicators, the examples below are merely a starting point. You are welcome to refute or confirm each with your own observations.

As with indicators, one or more of the following may apply to you; any which apply to you are completely within your control to change if you choose to. Our behaviours are largely the result of our choices, at least until they become habits. Sometimes just knowing that makes all the difference.

Driving: Naturally, not all drivers consistently reveal a lack of thought, just bad drivers. So who *are* these bad drivers? Most people see themselves as good drivers if not very good ones. Is everyone who believes they are good drivers correct?

The words *bad* and *good* are polar opposites in meaning. They are also somewhat useless; each describes qualities that are subjectively assessed. A novice tennis player might view almost everyone else as a good player until his own game improves. *Bad* and *good* are relative to whatever the person making that assessment thinks at the time.

When one driver judges another as bad, the judging driver believes the other one is bad in *comparison* to him. That implies that the judging driver believes *he* is a good one. Yet how many drivers believe *they* are bad ones, either by skill or practice, judged against a fixed standard or against the skills of other drivers? I suspect the number is very small. Recent research suggests that too.

Search your own recollections for the number of people you have heard say they are bad drivers. Compare that with the number you recall saying they are good drivers, or who judge other drivers as bad, thereby implying they are at least better drivers than the ones they judged. I can count on one hand the people I have heard refer to themselves as bad drivers. That's only my experience and knowledge but there's more.

Based on *Britian's Worst Driver*, *Canada's Worst Driver* (*CWD*) ran for nine seasons on the *Discovery Channel*. *CWD* featured a collection of really-bad drivers put through a series of driving instruction and challenges. The contestants were judged by a panel made up of a police officer, a senior driving instructor, a psychologist, and a former race-car driver. Each week, the best of the worst graduated until the worst of the worst remained. At the time of this writing (2013), a new show is underway wherein the worst drivers from those nine seasons face each other to avoid the dubious distinction of being *Canada's Worst Driver Ever*.

The concept was brilliant and the driving truly frightening. Viewers could glean all sorts of useful driving tips from the show, making it informative to watch. Each driver was nominated by a friend or relative who accompanied their nominee on the program. Few of these contestants accepted that they were truly bad drivers when they started; often just the opposite. Furthermore, we only saw the contestants who *agreed* to be on the show or whom the show's producers believed would engage viewers' interests. I can only imagine the number of bad drivers who told their nominators to piss off or who the producers rejected.

Another telling aspect of *CWD* was how diverse the drivers were. They varied in age, race, skin colour, religion, sexual orientation, driving experience and, yes, gender. I saw super geeks and guys who looked like Hells Angels, young bubble heads and nice grandmothers, city slickers and country bumpkins. I suspect the producers sought a varied mix. There seemed to be enough bad drivers from every conceivable group to allow ample diversity for every season. Equally varied among contestants were the errors when driving: too fast, too slow, too oblivious, too confident, too nervous, and too distracted. You name it, it was demonstrated on CWD if it was a driving mistake.

How would *you* have stacked up on *CWD*? Do you cut other drivers off? How many at-fault accidents or traffic tickets have you had? Do you merge properly? Do you share the road, or do you view it as your own personal domain that is rudely cluttered with less-important drivers in your way?

The Sun Group of Newspapers recently published their list of the 10 Worst Cities in the world to Drive In. My current home of Toronto is rated the 6th worst. No other city in the Americas (north or south) made the list except 10th place Los Angeles. The volume of Toronto traffic was cited as a leading issue with 70% of locals choosing to drive to work. Having North America's busiest highway can't help either. Nevertheless, there are cities with far more drivers, cars, bottle necks, and weather hazards. Having lived in Toronto for over 20 years, I'm convinced that bad drivers contribute to this dubious distinction, one I don't dispute one bit. This isn't to say most Toronto drivers are bad, that any other city's drivers are better, or that I'm a great driver myself. I suggest that bad drivers make driving worse for good ones, and that some bad drivers inspire good ones to join their ranks. The roads I travel daily provide examples by the truckload.

We all see bad drivers in action. They don't merge at the first sign of their lane ending, rather at the last possible moment, thus forcing other drivers to slow or stop to avoid collision. They drive slow in the fast lanes or fast in the slow ones. When stuck in traffic, they abandon their lane for a soon-to-end lane, drive past dozens of other motorists and then bud into the same lane again. They ride your rear fender or change lanes so badly you almost hit theirs. They have side and rear mirrors yet see nothing but brake lights ahead of them. They turn left into the far right lane. They park as close to the store as humanly possible then take ten minutes to back out because they cannot manoeuvre their vehicles well in tight spaces. Presumably, they all passed a driver's test that included rules about yielding to the right, but they forget that whenever coming to a four-way stop.

Bad drivers' make daily choices that suggest neither the rules of the road nor the rules of physics apply to them. Their moves often reveal to psychologists a personality change wherein they treat their vehicles as impregnable suits of armour that are part of them. None of those beliefs are true and, I suspect, few bad drivers consciously foster them. They merely drive in ignorance, doing things they never would as a pedestrian because others would call them on it or intentionally knock them down. In that way, bad drivers reveal a level of ignorance consistent with the worst piles of crap.

Laziness: We already looked at ignorance and how mental laziness plays a significant role in that. Physical laziness also reveals a susceptibility to crap.

We all have our lazy moments and days. We can all feel mentally and physically tired, although not all of us do anything before getting those feelings. Lazy moments can be quite healthy. Still, lazy moments are in the minority for those people least susceptible to piles.

By contrast, some people are lazy by habit because they simply don't think. How many people do you see litter streets with cigarette pack wrapping, a tissue, a gum wrapper, or a coffee cup? I could understand someone wanting to rid himself of plutonium. With common litter, though, why not stuff it in a pocket until at the next available trash container? Because these people simply don't think about it.

The same goes for people who leave their cars running for several minutes when in a convenience store, or waiting for their kids to come out of the local school. There are by-laws in many jurisdictions to curb what is commonly referred to as *idling engines* and a host of environmental studies that provide reasons for those by-laws. Yet many drivers ignore these laws and the reasons for them, or they are ignorant of them. I understand the need to idle an engine when it is painfully cold or oppressively hot, to run the heater or air conditioning in the car, but far more often it is merely the lack of thought that results in such non-choices.

Most kids could use much more exercise than they currently get. They could stand to walk a half block to a proper parking location and a switched off car. Mom or Dad could park a distance away and meet the kids out front. Plenty parents could use a little walk too, but they would have to think about that for a microsecond first, wouldn't they?

I remember speaking to one woman not long ago. She was sitting in her idling car, which was shaking due to the pounding bass of the stereo blaring within it. She was parked opposite an elementary school on a busy street her kid (or kids) had to cross in order to reach the dance club, I mean car. The school provided parents parking off the street so that the little ones wouldn't have to cross the street, which was narrow and provided insufficient room for school buses to manoeuvre if any cars were parked on it. Being the outspoken goof I am, I pointed that out to the woman when she opened her window. "I'm not the only one doing it", she spewed out, "so why should I move?" I couldn't help but think back to the pothead girl and steroid monkey: *everybody's doing it.* Presumably, a United Nations forum on illegal parking would be required, followed by rounds of negotiations, before she would stop exposing her own kid(s) to danger and rendering school buses unable to operate in front of her kid's school.

Few people who are this lazy are willing to put thought into whether or not they are being fooled by some poop speakers. Nor do they recognize their own poop when it crosses their lips.

Prejudice: In recent decades, we have all heard what I call *the isms.* They include *racism, classism, sexism, extremism,* and a host of words to which *ism* doesn't really belong but to which it is attached anyway. *Isms* usually describe behaviours or attitudes that are inaccurate or morally wrong, that are the cause of mistreatment of one sort or another. These words, the real ones and the made-up variety, fall under the term *prejudice,* which accurately describes all the isms and so much more.

Prejudice virtually always stems from ignorance and a lack of reasoned thought, most often passed on in the form of malignant piles. Racism is merely the most referred to kind. Not only does prejudice short change those who are painted with its very wide brush, it deprives those who do the painting of being in touch with good people who they could work with, live with, and learn from.

Take for example prejudice against certain professions. Some people don't trust doctors even when they need the attention of one, thus suffering needlessly. The best guy or girl for a particular job might be this skin colour or that, be of this religion or that. None of that should matter yet some people let it matter.

Ironically, some people rail against one type of prejudice yet demonstrate one or more brands of it themselves. Is some prejudice useful and fair while other kinds are not? Some racial advocates brand just about every one who disagrees with them as racist. Every group has their crosses to bear, but those idiots are usually the minority within any group and reflect badly on the rest through their bad actions. Such bad actors spawn stereotypes. As a colleague once asked, *how do you think a stereotype becomes a stereotype, anyway*? If stereotypes are inaccurate and bad in some instances, that principle ought to apply across the board, shouldn't it? As for lumping everyone of a certain skin colour or ethnic background or religion together, isn't *that* prejudiced?

I happen to have white skin. I had no more choice in that than in my height or eye colour. It stems from my parents genes. I hate it when some idiot speaks on behalf all *white people.* White folks have been kicking the snot out of each since there *were* white folks. Historically, people with other skin tones have done the same with similar-looking neighbours. White people vary widely in values, religious beliefs, language, customs, history, physical characteristics, and much more. So do South Asians, East Asians, Africans, and every other imaginable racial group.

I had to shake my head a few years ago when a group of disadvantaged youth from Africa, who happened to have dark skin (hence, they were viewed as 'black' by some people), were channelled by a city organization into a basketball program, presumably because all black kids like basketball. The kids were from Somalia, where soccer is king. They shook their heads too, with good reason. Apparently, even the best-intended city officials can reveal prejudicial piles too.

Political Correctness: For those unfamiliar with this term, there are several definitions provided below from the internet (sourced in brackets), each which touches on some aspects of *PC*:

- Avoidance of expressions or actions that can be perceived to exclude or marginalize or insult people who are socially disadvantaged or discriminated against (wordnetweb.princeton.edu/perl/webwn)
- Political correctness (adjectivally, politically correct; both forms commonly abbreviated to PC) is a term which denotes language, ideas, policies, and behavior seen as seeking to minimize social and institutional offense in occupational, gender, racial, cultural, sexual orientation, handicap . . . (en. wikipedia.org/wiki/Political_correctness)

- The concept that one has to shape their statements (if not their opinions) according to a certain political dogma, i.e. to be politically correct; the result or product of being politically correct (en.wiktionary. org/wiki/political_correctness)
- A trend that wants to make everything fair, equal and just to all by suppressing thought, speech and practice in order to achieve that goal. (www. information-entertainment.com/Politics/polterms. html)
- Suppressing the expression of certain attitudes and the use of certain terms in the belief that they are too offensive or controversial. (www.slp.duq.edu/ rentschler/ETHIC/Vocabulary.htm)

Since prejudice in any form sucks, is political correctness the opposite of prejudice? On the contrary. Stand-up comedians draw on a variety of topics to make fun of. Some choose politics and social commentary for their material. They include Scottish comic and actor Billy Connelly, who refers to political correctness as *the language of cowardice.* Another is American comic and commentator Dennis Miller, who refers to PC as *inverted McCarthyism.*

McCarthyism was a movement in the United States in the 1950s during which Senator Joe McCarthy's "House Committee on Un-American Activities" tried to find communists and their sympathisers in several occupations including entertainment and publishing. Even well outside Washington, the overall effect of McCarthyism was a culture of fear that saw many writers and teachers *blacklisted.* Employers and publishers avoided contact with such people lest they get blacklisted too. Anyone who appeared even a bit left wing was fair game.

Like McCarthyism used to, PC creates a culture of fear and intellectual intimidation, although mostly against the right wing of the political spectrum. People are expected to speak and act a certain way or risk being branded a racist, homophobe, sexist, class snob, and the like. As Billy Connelly's points out, PC forces those who follow it to be so bland and vague as to say almost nothing of any use.

In my view, PC promotes all sorts of poop by causing people to focus not on what they think but on what they believe is *safe to say*. If someone makes a whole range of assumptions about you based on a particular word or phrase you use, how are those assumptions not prejudiced unless the word is truly offensive by a reasonable standard?

Take race for example. I dislike racism because it is a form of prejudice and I hate words that racially offend, such as the dreaded *N word*. However, not every word that describes a particular racial or ethnic group is racist. Because language evolves, words and their use evolve within it too. *Oriental* is currently on an unwritten taboo list at Toronto City Council whereas *Asian* is the approved term. Never mind that Afghanistan, Turkey, China, India, most of the Arabic world, and a large chunk of Russia are all within Asia. Describing someone as Asian seems sort of useless then, doesn't it? In fact, if you describe someone as Asian looking, a Canadian or American might picture someone who looks like they are ethnically descended from countries like China, Korea, or Japan, whereas a Brit would more likely picture someone ethnically descended from India. Is it any less useless to describe someone as European or African or South American? How many ethnic, cultural, religious, historic, and language differences exist within those continents?

Consider Christmas time, er, I mean the *holiday season*. Because Christmas is historically a Christian thing, it is considered in PC terms as highly offensive to non-Christians. *Happy Holidays* and *the holiday season* are the approved PC phrases, at least this month. Regardless, a growing number of non-Christians, such as women wearing *hijabs* for instance, have greeted me with a *Merry Christmas* when I greeted them far less offensively. Why? I suspect it is because plenty of non-Christians understand how meaningful Christmas is for *us*, in religious terms for practicing ones and in good will for nominal ones like me. That's why I wish my Jewish friends Happy Chanukah and acknowledge Ramadan to my Muslim friends. Non-Christians have no way of knowing on sight that I'm not Jewish or Bhuddist. Since there are more Christians than Jews world-wide, and Bhuddism is usually associated with East Asian cultures, these non-Christians probably play the odds when they see a white face. Of course, I could get twisted up about that guessing but instead I appreciate the effort.

If at least a fair number of supposedly delicate non-Christians aren't offended by the mention of Christmas, who is then? The most predominant group of PC pile pushers are Christian, white-skinned, heterosexual males who take it upon themselves to decide what will offend everyone else. Is it just me or is that not a bit patronizing to every other group?

Despite very good intentions within most of our species, humans are complex and conflicted within our selves let alone with our neighbours. Misunderstandings arise all the time between people, even within families or groups who share much in common. Let's work through it and move on without prejudging what goes on when that happens. There are several groups whose culture and customs I don't understand, at least not yet. I don't have to understand everyone to peacefully co-exist with them. I have gay friends even though I don't understand how or why they are gay. I see eye to eye with these friends on many issues, so who cares? Some of my friends cheer for the Boston Bruins (hockey club), which I find far more curious, and far more of a choice.

PC doesn't stop offence from happening. To suggest it will is to shovel with the worst of them. P C merely chooses *whose* offence matters more. To label anyone who doesn't follow PC as being less tolerant is prejudiced. Besides, some people are simply more frank or plain spoken than others. Good for them! When potentially-harmful beliefs arise, do we want those hidden to fester without challenge, or do we want them brought into the light and challenged?

For all those reasons and many more, I believe PC=BS.

Reality TV: I referred earlier to *Canada's Worst Driver*, a show within a genre known as *reality-based television programming* or *reality TV*. By its name, one might think reality TV comes as close to the truth as any news program. Not so.

First of all, commercial television is driven in large part by money, as almost all business ventures are. That's not a bad thing, but it makes program producers want to put bums on couches to watch their programs and, more importantly, to watch the commercials during breaks in those programs. Producers try to create conflicts and potential dramas to achieve that. Accordingly, many reality TV shows are managed to a considerable extent, from casting to many other factors. Check out a few book titles on reality TV and see for yourself.

Reality TV shows are no more equal in quality than athletes are equal in talent. A show can provide some chuckles and surprises and insight, all in one package. Whether *CWD* or the *UFC* training seasons, some reality shows provide emotionally-healthy servings to their viewers. Some other shows, not so much. I don't have to watch Jerry Springer to know it's a bad and repulsive idea to bed my brother's wife and her mother and maybe my niece. Big Brother, the Bachelor/Bachelorette shows, and many others offer little more value than Jerry and his whoop-whoop peanut galleries. Should they be banned? Not at all. Are they walking, talking revelations of a strong susceptibility to poop think? You bet.

Canadians: "What?" You may think, "Are you even slamming your own people now?" Not all of us, but some.

In his satirical book *Why I Hate Canadians,* Canadian author Will Ferguson pointed out the juncture at which we collectively became *too* nice. It was when we decided it was okay for one of our provinces to separate if the majority there decide that they really, really want to. Never mind that it is the second-largest province and connects other provinces on its east and west borders. Ferguson is no more anti-Quebec than I am. I love the place and the overwhelming majority of its people. I feel better knowing that when the odd *separatiste* calls me a foreigner Quebec is still part of Canada. It's kind of difficult, though, to be taken seriously as a country when we're okay with a middle chunk of it flirting with breaking away, and when we pay the salary and pension of federal politicians who promote national separation. I suggest you make a list of all the other countries doing that. Done already? It's a bit like making breakfast for the guy who bedded your wife last night.

I don't advocate tossing separatists out of Parliament. That would be *rude*. But, no wonder some Americans don't take us very seriously, which brings me to the more troublesome aspect of Canadians as it pertains to poop think.

Far too many Canadians define us by not by what we *are* but what we *are not*, namely Americans. Our presumably shy folks are none too shy when it comes to slamming Americans, as often and as much as they can. *That's* nice. This brings me to yet another point. Some Canadians aren't nice at all. They believe we all are, to such an extent that some of us chastise other nationalities left and right for being nowhere near as nice as us.

With a friend from England, I recently slid up to a bar in the Dominican Republic. Two young women stood nearby and I simply *had* to know where they were from. Just two days before, I had seen one of them slug the other in the hotel lobby before a long screaming match seen by dozens of guests and staff. They seemed much calmer now, so I briefly chatted with them to learn where they were from. I wish I hadn't.

Not only are they Canadian but they live in Toronto, as I do. When they learned where I was from, the former pugilist said, "Yah, Canadians are the only nice people here."

"Hey, wait a second." I pointed out, "My friend here is from England." All these so-called ladies did was shrug, "Whatever". Nice! I was quite embarrassed, especially since my English friend, John, is way nicer than me. No BS, he really is!

To stake a national identity on not being like someone else seems a bit weak for me, not to mention pungent. The straw man fallacy is meant to get an opponent off the topic. The *at least we are not like them* angle is a version of that. To be selectively nice, to be faux-nice, or to be so nice you are a pain in the butt about it, well, that seems a bit stinky too. I don't know why we don't just fight amongst ourselves a lot more, like the nice American folks next door do. At least they're honest it.

Multitasking: I find it curious when someone tells me he is multitasking, which is to say I think it is crap. As with other poop revelations, multitasking isn't a crime. It is not evil. There will be no documentaries coming soon on the perils of it. Nonetheless, anyone who believes himself good at multitasking is swallowing his own poop. Yum!

Myth is often a polite term for poop, some myths so old as to be beyond easy fact checking. However, this particular myth is easy to prove as such. People who believe themselves able to multitask are not liars, but if they are human they are mistaken.

Multitask is a term borne out of data processing and computer science. It was used in relation to computers that can run two or more tasks simultaneously, and which are equipped with two or more *processors* specifically to run multiple tasks. While a brain isn't a processor and vice versa, one of the many functions each performs regularly is processing information, whether raw data or something more complex. In processing terms, a brain performs like the central processing unit (CPU) in a computer. Computers with lone CPUs *appear* to multitask but they don't really. In fact, they switch back and forth between tasks, albeit at ridiculously-high speeds. This creates the *illusion* of multitasking. Seasoned computer users know that applications function slower on single processor computers when more than one is running at once.

People can switch tasks too, which they *must* do when they perform more than one function during the same time period. But, we can't switch with the speed or accuracy of a CPU. Many moms and a growing number of dads cook breakfast, groom themselves, tell the kids to hurry up, tell the dog to stop barking, make a few calls to friends, maybe lament the lack of *nooky* since the kids came along, complain about the local team losing the previous night, or how overly friendly the dry cleaner's daughter seems to be. In truth, though, these folks only do one thing well at a time. They merely switch their attention as the bacon and eggs cook, the kids meander, the dog does what he does, and the dry cleaner's daughter, well, let's leave that one alone.

The more mindless or unconscious the activity is, the easier it appears for us to be able to do while doing something else. That is true to some extent, but with a twist. In his book *Crazy Busy,* Dr. Edward M. Hallowell provided what he called *Strategies for Coping in a World Gone ADD.* This guy knows a thing or three about actual Attention Deficit Disorder and co-wrote one of the leading books on that condition. *Crazy Busy* is mostly about self-imposed ADD, what I refer to as *Acquired Attention Deficit Disorder,* which people tend to show signs of when they try to do everything at once.

Hallowell provided several keys to his strategy, the second of which was finding your rhythm. He learned that tactic while working as a short order cook in a greasy spoon for a summer when he was twenty one. As he explained, there was no way to do everything from preparing every food station (hash browns, for instance) to waiting on every customer, filling every salt shaker, all at the first second that was required and throughout his shift. Once he found his rhythm, though, he was able to manage. He worked out an almost mindless routine for getting regular tasks done, set aside chunks or time for customers, another chunk for routine chores and clean up, that sort of thing. If a customer wanted coffee, he might get there in five seconds or a few minutes depending on what Hallowell was doing at that time, depending on where he was in his rhythm. Although he didn't describe it that way, Hallowell gave up trying to multitask, instead organizing himself into a workable routine where things got done.

Realizing we cannot multitask can be a great relief. Reworking how we do things to avoid trying to do what we cannot truly do anyway can be equally refreshing. Some tasks, however, do not mix well with each other no matter what some people believe. Boiling eggs or shaving are routine tasks that are somewhat mindless so you can do other things. Little will change in that routine from one minute to the next. *Everything* changes when it comes to, for instance, driving. From weather conditions and lighting to road conditions and everyone else's driving, things can change in an instant. Now throw in the very conscious task of having a conversation on a cell phone, hand held varieties being even worse. In the battle for your conscious attention, something has to give, and give it will. Of course, lots of drivers believe themselves so skilled that they add more tasks while chatting, perhaps smoking a cig, balancing a piping hot coffee, fiddling with the onboard GPS or all three, which combined with driving and yapping becomes *five* tasks. I've even seen a woman apply mascara while barrelling down a highway at 140 kilometres an hour. Have a nice drive!

The next time someone mentions multitasking, take a sniff and see what hits your nose.

The revelations above are merely samples. As with indicators, there are plenty more. They may appear to you as little more than me ranting on my personal soap box. My list is a lot bigger than what I provide above. You may see my choosing of examples far more stinky than the actual examples themselves. Despite citing some sources for verification, I make a number of suppositions I cannot prove without lots of additional study and work, if they can be proven at all. I may be wrong in all sorts of areas. Plenty of well-meaning people make mistakes and I'm no smarter or better than most.

With all that said, my examples are not BS simply because I put considerable thought into each one. In fact, my issue with each revelation is the thought absent susceptibility to poop think they each reveal. Someone can be wrong on any number of topics but by thoughtful consideration, I avoid poop talk by providing others with a way to prove me wrong, if and where I am.

Of course, these revelations and others like them aren't necessarily life and death stuff. Or are they? Naturally, *bad* driving can also be *dangerous* driving. Laziness can result in poor health habits as well as the very kind of physical inactivity that contributes to many health problems from heart disease to adult onset (Type 2) diabetes, to name just two. More broadly, many revelations, including those I provide above, stem from a lack of thought, essentially not paying attention.

In many ways, people who don't pay attention unwittingly rely on *other* people for their wellness and even survival. The night before I first drafted this chapter, a guy dressed all in black and chatting on a cell phone crossed four lanes of rain-slicked, busy traffic in front of me without a glance one way or the other. Neither I nor the dozens of others who were paying attention hit him but it would have only taken one driver being momentarily distracted or wondering out of his lane or previously having a few cocktails for things to change in a split second. In other settings, people depend on others to not punch them out when they bud into line ups, or not start a road rage incident when they bud into traffic lanes.

Fortunately for such thoughtless people, they have the capacity to change and in the mean time, a lot of good people who pay attention prevent these dunderheads from what Darwin referred to as the process of natural selection. There is a term for animals in the wild that don't pay attention: food.

My approach to poop aversion is not academic or technical. Poop busting can, actually, be child's play. I watched a news report recently about panda bears being lent to two Canadian zoos over the next several years. One enthusiastic boy of perhaps ten smiled brightly as he spoke to a TV news reporter. He was thrilled. As he explained with enthusiasm *and* precision, "In my opinion, panda bears are the greatest bears in the world."

This earnest boy may be right or wrong about pandas. Certainly *greatest* is difficult to argue. Still, even at his tender age, this boy was so well spoken that he made it clear he wasn't claiming anything, merely expressing his opinion. Very few children consciously compose their words or weigh out their later effect, especially when they're as excited as this lad was. Hence, the term *out of the mouths of babes.* When a ten-year-old child speaks with enough effortless clarity to avoid misunderstanding, even when nothing rides on what he says, doesn't it make you wonder why more people don't?

Even if you disagree with my assertions above, that disagreement requires your thought and consideration, the very stuff that stops poop in its tracks. When it comes to ranting, no one does it better than previously mentioned comic Dennis Miller. He has even done a few books with nothing but his rants. Opinionated though he is, he ends each one with the same honest disclaimer, "'Course, that's just *my* opinion. I could be wrong." I could be wrong too. Am I?

LIES

Any examination of BS requires a consideration of actual lies. Although they differ greatly from BS, lies are somewhat similar too. Many people believe they are the same, and you may have too before opening this book. By now, though, you have a solid grasp of the differences and similarities between these two forms of misinformation. Because actual lies are at the heart of some poop, if not much of it, let's look at actual lies for a few minutes.

Suppose someone told you that he heard your wife was stepping out on you, so to speak. Even the most hedonistic among us might see that as unwelcome news. Nevertheless, would that news be true, poop, or an outright lie? A few steps would help you determine if you should pack your bags, pack your wife's bags, or kick the guy speaking to you *in* the bag. Still, how could you *think* after your emotions were sent racing by that kind of news?

When faced with news of any kind from another person, a good place to start is with intent, often made easier by considering the source. Who would this guy be? He might be someone you have known for years as wholly reliable, someone you could trust with your life. Consistent with his character, he might have been trying to help you, having already sifted through someone else's potential BS to the best of his ability. On the other hand, he could be a rumour monger who valued your feelings and friendship about as much as you value the case of beer in your fridge; you enjoy it when it's there and move on the second the empties have nothing more to offer.

Credibility flows naturally from intent when it comes to information. Who wants to lie to a friend? Can a well-intentioned person be wrong, though? You bet. Where would he have got that big scoop from? Was the person telling you an effective poop sifter? A friend can have great intentions and still be a sucker for crap of all kinds. Even if you believed you could trust *your* source, you would have to remember that person is only the source for *you*.

Unless he was the guy going out with your wife, she confessed to him, or your friend saw your wife with another man (or woman) in a manner that could not be mistaken for something less upsetting, your friend would have at least one source too, the intentions and historical accuracy of whom would matter as well. You might have had to repeat this step a few times, if this scenario were real, but when an issue is important it is worth the effort. The same importance, for instance, could be attached to any number of other aspects of your personal, professional, or community life. At the end of the trail, sometimes there is fire where someone smelled smoke, sometimes all that exists is an innocent misunderstanding spun out of control by rumours or outright lies.

Although some spouses might be tempted to greet news of potential infidelity by shooting the messenger ("You're a liar!" might be one such shot), unwelcomed information is not necessarily a lie. Incorrect information isn't necessarily a lie either.

For something as simple as a lie, identifying one can be remarkably difficult. Moreover, branding someone a liar, or all unwelcomed information as lies when you don't know *that* to be fact is itself BS. As we have seen already, through my words and Professor Harry Frankfurt's:

- When someone tells you something true, he's being truthful.
- When someone tells you something untrue but believes it is true, that person is honest but mistaken.
- Only when someone tells you something untrue and knows it is untrue, is that person lying.

As Frankfurt explained, what truly sets lies apart from BS and other untruths is *knowledge* of the truth. If someone knows the truth and says something else, he is lying. If he doesn't know the truth, he *can't* be lying.

Of course, many piles BS originate as actual lies. An originating lie can morph into poop the instant it is accepted as true by someone who doesn't know better, or who doesn't care to know better.

Who cares about this subtle difference? In what world does this stuff really matter? Well, it matters in politics, law, law enforcement, medicine, education, the news media, dealing with friends and lovers and neighbours, and just about any potential relationship between people, whether directly or indirectly. Other than that, it doesn't really matter much.

Because it is so often difficult to *know for certain* what someone else knows, it is equally difficult to know when someone is lying. By comparison, it is fairly easy to detect fallacies, to recognize common or repetitive BS, to know you have the most truthful and accurate information in a given dialogue or debate. This is why so few people call everyone they disagree with a liar, even when they suspect someone *may* be lying. After all, to call someone a liar or brand something as a lie when you don't *know* either is true is no better than BS. It may be an educated guess based on someone's history as a liar, but even the best guess is a guess, which by definition falls well short of factual knowledge.

Proven liars, and even maniacal monsters, still tell the truth from time to time and they are correct or wise from time to time. For example, Adolf Hitler praised early versions of the Volkswagen Beetle as ingenious when it came out in 1933 and pushed to have it brought into mass production. Many decades of production and sales of the Beetle all over the world, as well as many design elements from that model being incorporated into other car models, show how right Hitler was in that regard at least. On the flip side of that coin, Hitler praised German engineers for the Beetle design whereas the true creator of the Beetle and its many innovative improvements over designs of the day was Josef Ganz, a Jew who narrowly escaped probable assassination by the Nazis. As Paul Schilperoord, wrote in *The Extraordinary Life of Josef Ganz—The Jewish Engineer Behind Hitler's Volkswagen*, Ganz, who had worked as a consulting engineer for Mercedes Benz and BMW, was jailed and persecuted by the Nazis, and was luckily on holiday in Switzerland when Nazi authorities came to his door to arrest him (again). Even the car's name came from Ganz, who first called it the *Maikäfer* (May Bug). My point is simply to say that in our search for truth we must be prepared for it to come from the most unsavoury people even while we remain understandably suspicious of what they say. If, for instance, the worst person you know of came running past you in a building and saying the building was about to blow up, you would be foolish not to heed that information, and the truth would emerge soon enough anyway.

That people often hesitate to call each others liars in vigorous debate is a good thing for civilized society, which offers plenty of piles without everyone calling everyone else a liar too. In some regions, that hesitance may save lives. Where guns are prevalent among average citizens, *shooting the messenger* could be quite literal if they went about calling each other liars without reasonable cause.

To see exactly what I mean about restraint in calling someone else a liar, watch a news program that features topical discussions between people of opposing views, or watch debates between campaigning candidates. These discussions may lack manners, logic, sometimes civility, yet the *liar* label rarely comes out. That doesn't mean a man or woman arguing one position doesn't suspect the other of lying, only that he or she can't prove it, or doesn't want to harshly label a verbal opponent. In other cases perhaps, someone may not want to call out an opponent as a liar lest he or she be similarly revealed that way some other time.

Looking back at benign BS, there are also instances of *benign lies*. Many people refer to them as *white* lies, but racial arguments and political correctness make that term a bit suspect. Benign lies provide an excellent example of how close lies can be to benign droppings.

Consider your imaginary friend Glen, worrying about how bad his food is going to be that evening. If you *knew* how bad his food would be, if you had sampled his cooking many times before and been nauseated by it, it would be an outright lie to tell him you were sure it wouldn't be. Be that as it may, the purpose of your lie would be as benign as if it were a benign dropping. Human feelings would be spared in either case. Provided you didn't tell everyone else how good Glen's cooking is, your benign lie would not morph into a malignant pile.

Once in a long while, someone spits out a less-benign lie that you know is a lie and that you can prove is a lie. In those instances, it can be enormously satisfying to out that person. It can be as liberating as an *actual* poo. When a liar is *outed*, he has the choice of walking around with his credibility in tatters or changing his approach to the truth. With the exception of those who compulsively lie, most liars can fix their ways. Some people have insufficient training or education or moral guidance to recognize the value of the truth. Such deficits can be fixed, although not with time or age.

Compulsive (or pathological) liars are another matter entirely. I won't pretend to have detailed knowledge about how compulsive lying occurs within the brain, which is to say I won't BS you. Nonetheless, I have experience dealing with two compulsive liars, for better and for worse. I referred to them concerning the BS indicator of being *never wrong*. Those experiences provided me excellent opportunities to observe such people's character, and to learn from my observations, many of them in hind sight after damage was done.

Compulsive liars are often personable and articulate. They are crafty enough to convincingly lie time and again. Fortunately, most compulsive liars seem to reveal a remarkably-simple *tell*, although I'm sure they don't mean to: compulsive liars almost never admit to anything negative being their responsibility. Whether it is a mistake or an omission, and no matter how trivial, it is always someone else's fault, never theirs. They will say and sometimes do almost about anything to avoid negative responsibility being assigned to them.

Accolades are no problem for such people, even if those are not due. On the other hand, fault is welcomed by compulsive liars about as much as sunlight would be welcomed by vampires (if they were real, I mean). This helps the rest of us spot them and consider them as sources. Just bear in mind that even compulsive liars, and the more-occasional variety of liars, sometimes tell the truth, as I pointed out above. With such people, corroborating evidence can help sift the truth. For example, if a person was previously convicted for perjury or otherwise shown to be untrustworthy, that person might still be shown truthful if sufficient independent evidence proved that. This is an important lesson captured in the old fable, *The Boy Who Cried Wolf.*

From my experiences and previous work, I know that people with significant skill deficits are more likely to avoid responsibility for bad things, in part out of habit. Therefore, they largely do it subconsciously. Because responsibility avoidance can be compulsive, so too can be lies to avoid that responsibility. However, responsibility avoidance as a result of skill deficits, at least in many cases I have witnessed, seems to differ from compulsive lying.

A lot of skill-deprived people who avoid responsibility *believe* they are unable to do anything different than they do, that whatever is wrong in their lives is completely out of their hands. Many of those people are programmed or trained that way through repetitive messaging, or an almost complete lack of thoughtful engagement. Very few dysfunctional people know what potential they have. Most don't believe they can make a positive difference. Some of those people don't care either, but that doesn't contradict their all too common lack of knowledge. On the same note, people in poor circumstances don't avoid *all* responsibility all the time, just the big-picture stuff. Whether you consider them skill deprived, dysfunctional, socio-economically disadvantaged, or something else, they are not necessarily liars, let alone compulsive ones, hence the significant difference. Such people have enough challenges without guys like me raining nasty labels on them.

By comparison, the two compulsive liars I knew each came from far more functional circumstances than I. Both were educated, well spoken, highly presentable, and very convincing. They effectively strung many people along for a long time, including me. One of them is now well known by former colleagues for the liar he is. The other is equally revealed and served a prison term I wish had been much longer.

There is also a potentially frightening aspect to people who display *some* of the traits I assign here to compulsive liars. Those traits are eerily consistent with those sometimes observed in psychopaths, both the serial killing kind and the much more common type, who are often highly successful in their jobs, personable, popular, and very effective at getting what they want, no matter how much that might cost someone else. Sometimes that behaviour results in crimes but in the vast majority of instances it *only* results in horrendous psychological damage to victims. Some employees are emotionally ravaged by their bosses for no reason other than sport. Some significant others are destroyed by emotional abuse, belittlement, sometimes financial ruin, that sort of thing. Some people are manipulated into all sorts of bad decisions or conflicts by people who cause that mayhem for their own amusement. Most psychopaths crave the rush that comes from seeing chaos erupt around them. For some of these folks, that chaos is a trail of bodies. For others, it is a trail of subordinates unfairly fired, or circles of friendships scattered to the wind.

The leading expert worldwide on psychopathy, both the clinical kind observed in some violent criminals and the sub-clinical kind operating within many social predators, is Professor Emeritus Robert Hare with the University of British Columbia's School of Psychology. He estimated that about 1% of the general population in North America are psychopaths, most who don't commit crimes whatsoever. Instead, these hidden monsters leave a trail of destruction within relationships, organizations, and companies.

In 1993, Hare wrote the widely-recognized *Without Conscience: The Disturbing World of Psychopaths Among Us,* which resulted from decades of research into convicted criminals, many of whom are *not* psychopaths. Hare pegged the in-prison psychopathy rate at about 20%. Hare, Paul Babiak (Hare's co-author of *Snakes in Suits: When Psychopaths Go To Work*), and Craig Neumann published a 2010 study of 203 corporate professionals, of whom nearly one in 25 (4%) qualified was "highly psychopathic".

In his article *Psychopaths Among Us* (Readers Digest, September 2011), George Binkie wrote that, "Attracted to positions of power, some of these individuals end up in law enforcement, the military, politics and medicine. Corporations are especially hospitable." Of course, the laws of averages and randomness suggest you may have absolutely no psychopaths in your work or personal world; some environments must be free of such monsters. On the other hand, the same law of averages could result in *more than* 1% of people within your environment, and perhaps more than 4%, being psychopaths. Comforting, isn't it?

As Binkie pointed out, "Robert Hare believes helping people to identify psychopaths, thereby reducing the risk of being victimized, is a public good". Whether they are serial killers, inter-office monsters, or domestic and/or child abusers, psychopaths are obviously serious business. I'm not suggesting for one second that all liars or even most of them are compulsive liars, let alone psychopaths. I mention the dark side of humanity simply to point out that people who frequently tell lies are a problem on their own, but in extraordinary cases those lies can be a symptom of something much more serious, and much less fixable.

I believe that helping people identify BSers is also a public good. I simply don't want well intentioned people to confuse BSers for occasional liars, compulsive liars, or psychopaths. These are all different issues with a variety of different solutions being applicable.

Just as there are BS indicators, there are also *lie* indicators, some which are beyond a liar's control. For clarification, most BS indicators can also work as lie indicators depending on the context of what is said and the situation where those indicators are tossed out. Other indicators, some which you may recognize yourself, seem to signal lies far more often than they indicate BS. They include such classics as *honest, I swear on my mother's/ grandmother's grave* and *As God is my witness.*

Experience and practice make the best poop busters *and* lie detectors so there is little need to delve deeper into that here. Practice may not make perfect, but it certainly makes a world of difference in both areas. That said, be careful not to swallow formula approaches to detecting lies.

There are many experts who stake their professional reputation on the accuracy of being able to spot lies based on such things as physical indicators. For instance, there is a common belief that the movement of someone's eyes in certain ways and directions indicates if they are lying or not. Many police officers and lawyers may believe in that formula. Extensive research, however, has completely debunked such formulas. Again, don't take my word for it. There is plenty of reputable research available to peruse at your convenience. It is the kind of research that increasing numbers of law enforcement agencies worldwide are tapping into in order to improve how they investigate crimes, which often involves interviewing people, some who lie to the police and others who do not.

In the world of untruths, BS is far more common if only because first-hand knowledge of the truth is far less common and necessary for a lie to be a lie. Such knowledge is rare in seemingly endless poop chains. Both BS and lies can be benign or malignant. Both have legitimate uses, although the more they are used, the less likely such use is either legitimate or benign. Honest!

MORAL QUANDARIES

After all the work you have done reading these past pages, and all the conscious thinking I have hopefully provoked, I am about to throw a monkey wrench into the works. Not for sport or enjoyment, and not to add a few pages to this intentionally-brief book. I do it to be truthful and to ask for a little help.

I am in a *quandary*, which is to say I'm uncertain about how to proceed with particular types of problems I explain shortly. There is a *moral* aspect to these, by which I mean ethics and principles come into play within these quandaries.

These problems concern the nature of people, not so much individuals but clusters of us. Over the past several years, I have spent considerable time and energy writing, lecturing, teaching, and thinking of ways to make the seemingly complex much simpler. That is the thrust of my previous work and this book, albeit to a lesser degree here. I take the same approach to some topics I teach.

In all those contexts, I repeatedly point out that simplicity and ease are two different animals altogether. I do so because the two are so often confused by many people. *Simple* is *uncomplicated* whereas *easy* is *not difficult*. If you ask a guy to pick up a piano, that's a simple request but by no means easy for any one person to perform. I also apply logic as a means of simplifying that which is initially complex. A logical approach to complex challenges is to break the latter down into more-manageable parts. NASA doesn't employ people and contract companies to build spacecraft. It employs or contracts teams of people to work out solutions to this small problem or that, build this component or that, and those collectively become spacecraft.

Throughout this book, I work to simplify an almost ever present aspect of life: BS. More or less, I think I have achieved that here and I believe most readers are capable of BS busting, for necessity or fun. So what's the problem, you may wonder. Well, people.

Individually, we can be highly thoughtful, inspirational beings who make the world a better place. More often than not, though, when put in large numbers we suck.

One might think people are smarter and better when put in large numbers. After all, a thousand brains can do a lot more thinking than one. When put in a focused environment like a research project or major undertaking, that is certainly the case. Most times, however, we seem to think less and do that less effectively when we are clumped in large numbers. The causes and the solutions, if the latter even exist, are neither simple nor easy.

Dealing with large numbers of people who cease to rationally think, either when connected by location or by collective decisions, can be difficult when you want to use any aspect of reason. I'll give you a well-publicised example from 2011. I like to watch hockey and grew up mostly in Vancouver, so I cheer for the Vancouver Canucks. That team lost the last game of the Stanley Cup final at home, disappointing most of their fans, including an estimated 140,000 plus people gathered in the downtown core who watched the game on gigantic screens set up by various sponsors. When the game and the Canucks' hopes ended, stupidity began in earnest.

Large mobs refused to clear the downtown core. Significant numbers took to breaking and looting. Fifteen cars, including two police cruisers, were smashed and set ablaze during what was quickly dubbed the *Vancouver Riots*. The city suffered a public black eye that left hundreds of people injured, millions of dollars in damage, and potentially many millions in lost tourist revenue. How could this happen, and not just recently but also in 1994 when the Canucks also lost in the Stanley Cup finals? Not just in Vancouver but other cities around the globe where such stupidity has played out on the grand scale? How and why?

The simple answer is that large numbers of people suck. A more-complex answer has to do with the dynamics of large crowds, which is well documented by researchers. Alcohol certainly played a role in dulling the wits of countless people, and I know first-hand how many anarchy bent folks spend their days and nights hanging around the Granville Mall near where the mayhem took place, and within walking distance of where I grew up. Still, plenty of seemingly regular folks participated and greatly outnumbered what some might dub *the usual suspects* in the downtown core.

Those who did the damage were probably in the minority, but a minority of well over a hundred thousand people is still a lot of bad actors. An even smaller minority tried to stop the mayhem, tried to protect people or property, but they were the exception. The vast majority neither caused the damage nor tried to stop it. Instead, they watched, took photos or video, posed with stupidity in the background, and even cheered it. This is similar to crowds standing around watching bullies beat a hapless victim, or standing around with their pitchforks centuries ago watching a group stone someone to death. That large numbers of people suck is nothing new.

How can reasonable individuals, or groups of reasoning people, affect the choices and actions of mobs? I'm not entirely sure, hence, this chapter. This quandary isn't limited to crowds of temporarily-hammered idiots either.

Consider how election campaigns work. People are not clustered together in one place and they are hopefully sober most of the time. Yet the voting choices of many citizens appear no more thoughtful than that of drunken mobs. Many voters base their choices on considerations that seemingly have little to do with the candidates they support. Campaigns post as many signs as they because experience indicates that name recognition can swing undecided voters when they arrive at the ballot box. Name recognition is hardly a reason to purchase a particular soap, let alone choose who represents you in government for the next few years. Daily opinion polls often sway voters in a momentum-generating wave even though it shouldn't matter to any voter who randomly selected telephone respondents say they will vote for. Some people vote for a candidate because of the party that candidate is lined up with. Others vote for a party because that's the way their friends or family have voted for years. Some voters support a candidate based on familiarity or because he or she looks like the same ethnic group as the voter. How are those choices any more mindful than car torching?

The same lack of thought goes into purchasing choices for millions of people, how they choose what television shows to watch or CDs to buy or movies to order on demand. These choices do not usually affect other people, not directly at least, so they seem less harmful than cars being flipped or poor representatives being elected. Still, the operative lack of thought exists across all these scenarios, as it does with a number of common problems from littering to traffic congestion. As I quoted Dr. Albert Schweitzer previously, "The problem with man today is simply that he doesn't think." No kidding!

So, what can reasonable people, like you with your new or perhaps-better-honed BS busting skills, do to make a difference? That too is a quandary.

I will give you an example from Canadian politics, because I'm Canadian. I have seen many similar examples in other countries too, and you may have as well. It is a widely held opinion among political pundits and journalists in Canada that Preston Manning may be the most intelligent, honest politician in recent history in Canada but he never became Prime Minister. Why?

Young Preston grew up in Edmonton as the son of Earnest Manning, Alberta's Premier for decades. The elder Manning was also an ordained minister who broadcasted to his flock every week on the radio. In time, the younger Manning formed a new political party and suggested political solutions that shook the status quo. He explained those well and often. Nonetheless, gains by his party were slow and small, and Manning was accused by some political opponents as being a religious zealot despite not being overtly religious himself. In time, that party changed its name and leader when Manning willingly stepped aside, and that newer party eventually merged to form the Conservative Party that won a majority in Parliament under the leadership of Stephen Harper, one of Manning's earliest followers. That transition happened, in my opinion, because as that party evolved it became more mainstream, a bit less idealistic. Put another way, it became a lot more *political.* None of these are judgements, merely observations. An old saying in politics is that there are two things people should never see made, laws and sausages. Politics is what makes laws.

It is possible, if not likely, that what won the election was a combination of compromising core principles and adopting mainstream political tactics. For fairness and comparison, the same can be said of the opposite end of the political spectrum, the New Democratic Party. None of this is to point fingers at the right or the left, it is merely to illustrate that strong ideas and principles valued by small groups are not always easy or even possible to sell to masses of voters. What is often required is salesmanship, *dumbing down*, or watering down the product to make it less scary to sometimes thoughtless voters.

Preston Manning's approach to politics and party building was a sharp departure from politics as usual. Like the best ideologue, he seemed to operate on a higher plain. Many observers agree on this even if they didn't agree with his opinions or policies. Did Stephen Harper with the Conservatives, and Jack Layton with the New Democrats, somehow sell out in order to get elected? I don't think so but like many uncertain matters, this can be considered a quandary. Political opinions aside, Stephen Harper and his Conservatives seemed to have been faced with two clear choices:

- Hold onto ideology and principles, probably in obscurity
- Play the game of elections, get elected, and execute *some* of that ideology

A strong argument can be made that without the Conservatives conforming to the game of elections as they are currently played, and to politics in general between elections, few if any of Manning's principles would have seen the light of day. By working within the deeply-flawed system that is popular democracy, things can arguably be achieved even if by messy means. Whether they are good things or bad things depends on your political beliefs or on history's telling. This particular moral quandary is by no means Canadian. The same kinds of choices face Democrats and Republicans in America, Tories and Labour in Britain, and many other parties in other countries.

Let's consider a far-more-individual and hypothetical example, seeking promotion within a large organization. It could be a large corporation or a branch of the government, say for instance the military. The promotional process within large organizations often requires candidates to conform to the wants of those in charge. Being free thinking, creative, critical, and logical can all slow the rise of the brilliant people in large organizations. Many of the best future leaders, the ones who think of others and not just themselves, seek to gain promotion within their organizations to make things better. That becomes a much more difficult task if the message one sends to his or her bosses is that if promoted they will do things much better than the *dunderheads* who steered the ship before.

Those who rise within flawed organizations, then, often compromise personal characteristics and principles to gain the opportunity to make things better, albeit to a lesser degree and a slower pace than they would prefer. In doing so, do such movers and shakers become sell outs or realists? Another moral quandary.

Let's look at an even smaller-scale scenario, parenting a teenager. I can personally tell you that is no easy task. How does a parent make a teenager understand why he or she must follow certain rules, respect certain boundaries? Through reasoning? Not usually. Although some teenagers become excellent at *reasoning,* and quite early in their game, most do not. This can be due to a lack of guidance, reasoning role models, emotional issues common to almost all teens, teen brain development, psychological growth, and many other variables. *Because I said so* is far from the ideal approach to get a teenager on board. *Or else* isn't much better. Be that as it may, sometimes that is the only option left for a parent to get his or her kid to do the smart thing, the safe thing, and right thing, the moral thing. Sometimes, then, the most effective way to get a teenager to do the smart thing is to abandon his or her moral commitment to reasoning, to finding and promoting the truth of matters. If such moral abandonment results in a teen *not* winding up pregnant, in jail, or dead in a drunk driver's car, can they be so bad? As I say from the outset, I'm not sure.

Having laid out such a potentially-depressing set of scenarios, I have a few suggestions that are simple but by no means quick or easy. Logic is neither of those either. For what those suggestions are, merely turn the page.

REASONABLE HOPE

Having laid out some definite and considerable challenges, and established that there is no limit to what I *don't* know, I have a few ideas. They may be good, they may not be good. I guess you will know better than I if they work. You will see what I mean shortly.

First, since large groups of people suck and they are very hard to reason with, don't try. Centuries of examples illustrate the hazards of trying to reason with large numbers of people being really stupid. Instead, try to break large groups into very small ones, even individuals if opportunities arise. Consider as an example a school where violence is increasing. Rather than address a large assembly of students where hundreds will ignore reason in order to appear cool or aloof to peers, you could try addressing classrooms or even small clusters of students instead. By helping small groups of youth understand the reason behind reducing violence everywhere, including schools, those students can then influence peers to understand that too.

Second, elevate those who show reasonable understanding of whatever the core issue is to positions of leadership or increased recognition. In a busy downtown core during a major event, that could mean giving some citizens a T-shirt or hat identifying them to the police as part of the solution, not the problem. That would also implicitly tell some potentially bad actors the *everyone is doing it* belief so many idiots subconsciously adopt is, as they can see, BS.

Third, get into the habit of consciously thinking and reasoning, inside your head to start with, outwardly as you get better at it. Because some people act a lot more like sheep than human beings, in large groups and small, habits are sometimes transferred from one person to the next. Not all the time but some of the time. Why not let some good acts catch on instead of just stupidity? This is the stuff of peer pressure. It need not work in only in negative directions.

Fourth, acknowledge and realize that there is an ever present battle within people's heads between their instinctive, emotional responses and their skilled capacity for reason. Within the biggest idiots, that battle may be nonexistent because of little or no reasoning capacity being within them, not yet anyway. Even the most reasonable people have emotions and can give into those, which is sometimes a good thing lest we all act like robots. To realize that reason and emotion exist, and that they often conflict, gives reasoning a fighting chance within one's brain.

Fifth, acknowledge that, sometimes, direct action without apparent reasoning is necessary to prevent lunatics from running the asylum. This is evident, for instance, when well-meaning police officers do apparently mean things in potential riot scenarios, or when an emergency room physician tells a patient she must immediately do a procedure that will hurt like a bastard but provides no explanation. There is little time for reasoning in circumstances that quickly turn violent on a street or potentially fatal in a treatment room.

Last but not least, consider how diseases and positive trends develop, how good and bad ideas gain traction.

It happens through a mathematical concept known as *geometric progression*. Author Malcolm Gladwell provided an excellent example in his best seller, *The Tipping Point:*

> Consider, for example, the following puzzle. I give you a piece of paper, and I ask you to fold it over and over again, and then again, and again, until you have refolded the original paper 50 times. How tall do you think the final stack is going to be? In answer to that question, most people will fold the sheet in their mind's eye, and guess the pile would be as thick as a phone book or, if their really courageous, they'll say that it would be as tall as a refrigerator. But the real answer is that the height of the stack would approximate the distance to the sun.

I first read that passage about a week before presenting to a group of students in what was then one of the most violence plagued middle schools in Toronto. I wanted to be sure of this concept before trying to sell it to a bunch of cynical 6th, 7th and 8th graders. So I took the scientific approach, much as they do on the television show *Mythbusters.* If my experiment worked, it would strengthen Gladwell's stated theory. If not, then I wouldn't use it.

I got the longest piece of regular paper I could find, albeit a slim one. I purchased standard rolls of cash register tape that were 125 feet long. I opened one roll, laid it out flat, and folded it in half as many times as I physically could, which was nine times. The stack was 38 millimetres thick. I then multiplied that number by two in order to get the thickness of another fold, and I hit the = sign on the calculator 40 more times to approximate 50 folds in total. The result was 83,562,883,710,976 millimetres. I then divided that result by 1,000 to arrive at metres and 1,000 again to arrive at kilometres:

83,562,883 (over 52 million miles, for those unfamiliar with the metric system). Then I did a little research on the distance between our planet and the sun, which varies widely depending on the time of year and where we are in the terms of orbital position. Still, it is tens of millions of kilometres (and miles), as would be the imaginary stack of folded paper, so theory confirmed.

If you had trouble imagining the correct kind of answer, join the club. You might wonder to yourself, who cares? Why does it matter? As Gladwell explained,

> As human beings we have a hard time with this kind of progression, because the end result—the effect—seems far out of proportion to the cause. To appreciate the power of epidemics, we have to abandon the expectation about proportionality. We need to prepare ourselves for the possibility that sometimes big changes follow from small events, and that sometimes these changes can happen very quickly.

Of course, other things can spread far and wide and very quickly too, such as the most malignant piles imaginable. Just as dangerous contagions spread much quicker now due to almost universal access to international flight, malignant piles spread much quicker due to the internet, 24-hour news channels and so on.

Geometric progression explains the increasingly popular term "viral", which often applies to the popularity of commercial products and entertainment productions, political beliefs, personal videos and, of course, ideas. Hopefully, a movement against malignant piles of BS will be sparked by you reading this book, consciously discussing your thinking, and getting others you know to take those first and second steps. Time will tell if that happens.

Geometric progression helps explain how riots happen and how dictators sometimes get lawfully elected before they shut down further elections. With that said, geometric progression need not be a scary concept. We need not ground all flights or disconnect the World Wide Web.

As Gladwell explained and as I stated early in this chapter, good things work the same way as bad. They too can multiply exponentially over short periods of time. I'm no math whiz. Because I could figure out, execute, understand, and illustrate geometric progression, it must be a simple concept and a simple fact. Naturally, that doesn't make it easy.

Contagious diseases spread exponentially well, in part, because they don't *think*, they just *do*. Bacteria don't worry about whether or not other bacteria will do their part to spread the disease; a bacterium does not have a brain. They just multiply over and over again, until or unless something stops them, such as the right medication to kill them, the conditions for them (such as extreme heat or cold) becoming inhospitable, or a host body dying with no live host bodies being available nearby for them to spread to.

While thinking is a great thing I advocate repeatedly, some could say *ad nauseum*, thinking oneself into a state of inaction defeats part of the purpose of BS busting, which is to make others think too. Sometimes, one must simply act, even if that act is merely speaking to people, engaging them in some way that will provoke thought and reasoning within them. Sometimes, we have to follow the well-known Nike commercial promotional phrase and *just do it.*

Looking at the topic of this chapter reasonably, dealing with large numbers of people (meaning idiots who suck) can be a daunting task. Yet as Gladwell's explanation of geometric progression and my simple-yet-scientific demonstration collectively suggest, progress can be made on this front too despite the overwhelming odds. People can lie but true science doesn't.

As the second-noted quote above from *The Tipping Point* stated, "these changes can happen very quickly." I'll give you an example and you can, if you like, run an experiment to prove or debunk my theory.

For my theory, I will choose jaywalking and the resulting fatalities. Every traffic accident in the developed world that results in serious injury or death is thoroughly investigated by police. Statistics from those investigations are often released to the public to educate us, provided we *think* that is. These statistics are readily accessible on the Internet.

American statistics indicate that a total of 4,881 pedestrians were killed in motor vehicle accidents in 2005, yielding a per capita death rate of 1.6 pedestrian deaths for every 100,000 people. Canadian government statistics indicate that pedestrian fatalities in the most recent period averaged 416 per year. Since the American population is estimated to be roughly ten times that of Canada, per capita statistics for each country seem similar then. These deaths, then, seem to have nothing to do with nationality, rather with bad decisions on either a driver's part or a pedestrian's part. Of course, many more collisions of this type result in injuries, which are also tracked.

In Toronto, the majority of pedestrian fatalities are reportedly the fault of pedestrians. The vast majority of these victims cross a road somewhere other than at an intersection, or they cross against the signals or signs at an intersection. These statistics can also be found elsewhere through local police agencies. Since the per capita statistics are similar across borders, it is possible if not also likely the at-fault rate for pedestrians is similar between these countries too.

Battling cancer takes years of research, billions in funding, and a little luck for those afflicted. The same thing goes for many other potentially fatal ailments. Deaths from natural disasters such as tornadoes, hurricanes, tsunamis, and earthquakes are somewhat preventable but also dependent on a lot of other people for resilient residences, infrastructure, early warning systems, training of citizens, and emergency planning to limit the number of fatalities when unpreventable natural disasters occur. By comparison, pedestrian fatalities appear wholly preventable at what some might call the *grass roots* level, the level at which single individuals can make a difference.

So, here is my theory on how to dramatically reduce pedestrian fatalities within your country within a very short time frame. That success can be measured by the change in those readily available statistics.

First, make sure you *only* cross main roadways at a crosswalk or intersection, and only when you have the right of way to do so, with the traffic lights or when the approaching car faces a stop sign or yield sign. I suspect that few if any dead pedestrians previously thought they would be killed, yet it happened. I'm confident that you don't believe you will be killed or badly injured as a pedestrian, yet I seriously doubt anyone else did who was later killed as a pedestrian. By taking this first step you can dramatically make your belief far more realistic and probable.

While this initially requires reasoned thought, it will become a habit. Several studies suggest that an average of 21 days of regularly practicing anything is required for a habit to take hold (for actions, not substances). That likely relates to nueroplasticity, the manner by which our brains rewire themselves through repeated actions or challenges. Once this first step becomes a habit, little to no conscious thought will be required most days to keep making that safer decision. Still, the benefits will kick in on day *one*, not day *twenty*-one.

Second, convince two people you know, whether friends, neighbours, family or peers, to do the same thing, and to similarly convince two other people to follow their example. And so on. That's it. Simple *and* easy.

Here's where the math kicks in:

Day 1:   one person (you)
Day 2:   two people (excluding you)
Day 10: 1,024 people
Day 20: 1,048,576 people
Day 25: 33,554,432 people (roughly the population of Canada)
Day 29: 536,870,912 people (well over the population of the United States)

In less than a month, you and a few friends, family, neighbours, peers, and millions of strangers could eradicate at-fault pedestrian deaths in your own country. Of course, many things could delay this progression. Some people who are approached by someone newly arrived on your bandwagon might already be on it, thus requiring that new arrival to find someone else not yet on board. Similarly, it is almost impossible to get everyone on board for anything. Nonetheless, even if not every living soul buys into your experiment, dramatically large numbers can make revolutionary changes. I'm not suguesting charitable donations here or anything so selfless and giving. This is self-preservation, along with preserving your kids, parents, and many others. Self-preservations is wired into our instinctive nature when internal BS doesn't interfere with it.

Bear three other facts in mind that could positively impact on this experiment, should you choose to take up the challenge. First, you may not be the only person in your country to read this challenge so the odds of success may be greater if even a few people take it up. Second, even if only one other person takes up the challenge that will cut the required time for achieving that lofty goal in half. And third, that challenge becoming reality needs only two things: 1) That one person to read this challenge, and you have already done that here, and 2) that one or more people take that challenge up.

There is one more aspect to this challenge. Aside from statistics, it will be easy to see how well it catches on by the simple observations of people around you on main roadways. If they follow your lead or do the smart thing in the first place, you will see the result. If some of them don't, you will see that too and you will have an opportunity to fix that if you choose, by approaching that person with the facts you have and your ability to reason. Your choices will be equally visible to other people, so if you only pass it on and don't follow your own words, that too will be evident. That has stopped more than a few parents, such as me, from some poor choices. No one likes to be called a hypocrite.

Naturally, pedestrian deaths might not get your attention as much as something else. If so, pick something *you* care about. It could be littering, parking in the wrong spots, driving while using a cell phone, wearing clothes way too tight or loose, profanity, whatever. Provided there is a way to see if others follow along, and others can see you doing that too, it is a somewhat measurable experiment even if statistics are not readily available to you.

Will you fail to evoke thought in other people if you try to? Well, *failure* is a subjective word meaning different things to different people. If you only view success as the spread of my idea on the same time table I provided above, failure is possible, perhaps even probable given how badly large numbers of people suck. Here is a rock solid fact, though: If you don't try, you are *assured* of failing.

Depending on many variables, from where you live to who you know to how outgoing you are to how much you buy into what I'm selling here, your chance of failure at this experiment might be 20% or 50% or 90%. If you don't do or say anything to get your experiment going, your chance of failure will be 100%, guaranteed. For future reference, I refer to this principle as *possible success versus assured failure.*

That principle is remarkably simple and easy to understand. It is also one that many people already follow without me and my label for it. Some young kids who appear to lack talent strive for success and stardom in a particular sport or art form. Many of them will fail at that goal, which isn't to say they will not benefit from the journey of trying, or find success in many other goals. None of those youth who *don't* try will ever succeed. Not one.

Many choices can increase the chances for success, thus decreasing the chance of failure. A kid striving for greatness in a sport, for instance, could eat right, rest well, work on physical fitness, train more and more intelligently than his or her competitors. A budding actor could read lots of plays, do memorization exercises, take extra classes on acting, and work on self-confidence through a variety of means. You get the idea. Therein resides what I refer to as *reasonable hope.* While hope is usually viewed as being blind or a long shot at best, it can also be reasonable. Because of what I describe above, not to mention what you may already know without me, hope can often be reasonable.

There is a basis for hope, sometimes based on geometric progression, sometimes based on the principle of possible success versus assured failure, sometimes based on something unknown within an individual's character that drives her to keep trying until she succeeds, at something if not the initial goal. None of this is because I say so, rather because science does. Who can argue with science? Well, anyone can. Reasonable, truth seeking science can withstand challenge. So prove me wrong. Try to make a difference and see where it takes you. If you do, please check out Appendix C.

T & E

I cryptically titled this chapter as I did to prevent readers from wondering, at the outset, why a book about BS finishes this way. T & E refers to Training and Education. Do you know the difference between training and education? And, what the heck has that got to do with BS anyway?

Training and education are the best defence against BS of any kind and, as it turns out, you have recently been getting both whether or not you did before, and whether you previously recognized that or not.

Education is defined as the process of imparting general knowledge, developing the powers of reasoning and judgement, and generally preparing oneself or others intellectually for mature life. I collect quotes and my current boss, Lydia Glavin, recently gave me an excellent one on this topic: Education teaches you *how* to think, not *what* to think. By comparison, *training* is defined as the education, instruction, or discipline of a person being trained. Although those may seem the same, education and training differ in an important way, especially as it relates to BS busting.

Education is widely viewed as a good asset for anyone. I agree. Who cannot benefit from education? Upon who is education wasted? Is a tradesperson, chambermaid, ditch digger, or stay at home mother unworthy of education? Such people are no less in need of sound reasoning and wise judgement than lawyers and business leaders. These are the same assets that allow us to detect and bust piles of all sorts. Although trades people, chambermaids, full-time moms, and other laypeople like me may be targeted by BS no more than any other groups, we are certainly targeted no less.

I know trades people, and know *of* many more, who are very successful by whatever means you measure success. Thus, you could argue that a formal education is nowhere near as valuable to such people as training in job related skills. That is true as it relates to their job skills yet incorrect once you consider how many other areas of life an education can be used for. The good news for tradespeople and many others busy earning a living is how achievable an education is.

Historically, *education* was considered a formal process and in many circles it is today too. *Formal* education is acquired through school, including post-secondary institutions such as universities. For those who can afford the time and expense, formal education is highly beneficial no matter what the educated person later does as an occupation. Nevertheless, there are other means by which one can acquire an education although rarely as structured.

Reading is one of the best means to become more educated or *self-educated*. Ideally, even formally educated people continue to learn through reading as well as through diverse experiences and exchanges. Although all manner of crap inhabits the Internet, there are useful and accurate sources of information there too. Self-education can be further enhanced through thoughtful choices in television and movie viewing and activities. For instance, many documentaries are very informative on an endless list of topics.

Some books, web sites, television shows, movies, and documentaries are heavily biased in one way or another, yet so too are many teachers and professors. Formal education is no guarantee against exposure to bias. Whether or not education occurs in school, an education ideally teaches one *how* to learn more and learn better throughout life. What you continue to learn can include additional job skills or different jobs, topics of interest, and last but not least, what the truth is in any given matter. In a nutshell, when you are educated, you are better equipped and prepared to repel BS of all kinds no matter how you prepared for such repelling. In fact, the little known term *autodidact* describes one who is self-taught to a significant degree, usually through vast amounts of reading, pondering, and application of that learning in various ways. Abraham Lincoln, for one, was an autodidact before he entered law school. That's the good news about education.

The bad news about education, and there is some, is similar to the bad news about poor drivers. You can know how to drive well and safely, drive a high-quality car on well-maintained roads, and still be a danger to yourself as well as others if you don't put those elements together. Why would someone know how to drive well, be well equipped to do so, and *not* drive well? Some people are overconfident in their initial driving abilities and soon after develop bad habits, believing that driving rules are intended for lesser skilled mortals. Others know just enough to pass their test but fail to practice the required skills to drive well. They fall to a much lesser level of performance when they are not consciously on their best behaviour. Others know better but drive badly, sometimes dangerously, because it is more convenient at the time, despite the danger they and their choices present to everyone else on the road.

All of these failings and many more can befall educated people when it comes to other aspects of life. Just as many bad drivers believe they are good ones because they have a license in their wallets, many people who show stupidity in aspects of their life believe they are universally smart because they have degrees on their walls.

Nothing about education makes one *more* vulnerable to BS, just the opposite. Yet some people who are provided with all the tools necessary to detect and destroy poop are instead crushed under its weight. Why? I suggest it is a lack of ongoing practice. Practice is required to turn new skills into habits. This is what educators refer to as *integration*.

When we do not integrate new learning into what we do, we often forget what that learning is, at least on some levels. Veteran educator and researcher M. David Merrill outlined his five *First Principles of Instruction*, stages of learning which make learning complete and without which learning is far less effective. Integration is the final step in his description of that process. It occurs when we connect what we just learned to what we previously learned, ideally in as many ways as possible. In that way, for example, a student paramedic who learns about head injuries will not only use that knowledge in his future job but also wear a helmet when he goes cycling, buckle up when he drives, make sure everyone with him buckles up when they are in his car, make sure his nephew's football coach gets a copy of the latest information on preventing head injuries, and when he has completed his formal studies he will read up on neuroplasticity's role in the recovery efforts for some head injury patients. In essence, this imaginary student would make it a habit to use and spread his new knowledge by training himself to use it, and perhaps training others through his insistence that they buckle up with him and so on.

The most beneficial element of training results from a form of discipline, namely *self* discipline. The most effective forms of training often include repetitive exercises or practices to instil habits. As with education outside of formal settings, training can also be achieved outside formal settings.

Sticking to the visual/virtual approach of this book, consider actual poop instead of the virtual type I so often refer to. We all poop with reckless abandon soon after making our noisy debut into the world. While we initially need to wear diapers, those of us with healthy functioning bowels learn how to control them so we can empty them when and where it is convenient, appropriate, hygienic, and far less embarrassing to do so. That transition starts with learning the *concept* of bowel control, but every parent knows there is a whole lot more involved with going potty than the concept. This process is commonly called *potty training,* not potty education. It takes time, failures, revisiting the concept, and endless parental patience. Slowly but surely, going potty properly becomes a strongly ingrained habit when sufficient guidance, correction, and reinforcement are provided us. Just as important, the thought of going potty in our pants ceases to be an option to us even though we *all* did that early in the game.

Training and its core tool of discipline work the same way in many other settings to meet many other needs. Whether for the military, medicine, policing, law, carpentry, baking, or any other profession, training is integral to success. Many trades are taught through apprenticeship, during which skills are taught and repetitively demonstrated, improved, and demonstrated again until the apprentice becomes a skilled, experienced, confident, qualified tradesperson. BS busting can be taught in various ways under various names yet without training and the hopefully constructive habits it enables, it can be hit and miss at best.

When it comes to knowledge, there are two distinctive kinds: *static* and *fluid*. Each is interdependent but their functions and value differ greatly depending on circumstances.

As the term suggests, *static knowledge* doesn't change. Although the amount and detail of our static knowledge can increase over time if we add to it, whatever we retain remains fixed unless we forget some of it. You either recall your mother's birth date or you don't. You know the capital of Uruguay or you don't. Even simple math problems can be *solved* through static knowledge, such as simple multiplication problems. As discussed in *Reasoning*, you probably know what three times six is because you retained that information in your memory from memorizing the multiplication tables, probably up to 12 x 12, as a child. You have static knowledge of those tables.

Fluid knowledge is flexible, changeable, adaptable, and widely applicable. Remembering multiplication tables is of little use when you need to know the result of 759 x 4,936. What yields an answer to that mathematical problem is a *process*. Reasoning is a process by which BS is busted, and that process can be difficult or second nature depending on how often and how effectively someone practices that, how much in the habit of reasoning a particular person is. In this math scenario, you know that process. To describe it would take a lengthy paragraph. You can probably perform that function almost automatically because you repeatedly did so for many years in school. If you have relied on calculators for years, that process may not be as readily available in your memory but it is still there, and you can come much quicker once you practice it again. Another term for a process is *procedure*.

The noun *process* describes a procedure or way that is used to figure a problem out or make a particular result happen. The verb *process* describes following a procedure or working through something, whether a set of thoughts into a conclusion in your head or a bunch of lumber into a desk in your workshop.

When it comes to our minds, there is more to them than mere knowledge and intellectual results. There are understanding and emotional aspects to some information. When a woman is told her husband has died in a car accident, she will hear that news and understand that hubby isn't coming home again, which is bad enough. As she processes that raw information and whatever details follow later, perhaps days or weeks or even months later, she will draw conclusions and formulate all sorts of thoughts that flow from the static knowledge she has. They will include what her feelings were for her husband and thousands of other variables. Moreover, all that processing will impact the lady's emotions, which is another process that differs from understanding her loss on an intellectual level. That is why when a person hears certain bits of news, whether good or bad, that person may need time to process that, intentionally or not, consciously or subconsciously.

Processes and procedures are used regularly by electricians, physicians, carpenters, soldiers, farmers, street sweepers, mothers, sport coaches, fire fighters, and hosts of others. They each require some amount of static knowledge, but it is the knowledge of *how* to process something, and previous experience in doing so, that often influences how successful the result is.

My point: Education and training are important for us all. There are formal settings wherein one can obtain these and several informal means through which one can as well. The end result of either way is, ideally, a good base of knowledge with which to navigate the various paths we take. Many of those paths will have unwelcome obstacles on them. We can step around those piles, throw them back at the source, or walk straight into them. It all depends on how well and accurately we navigate. Since navigation is a process, we are wise to practise that one and many others well in advance to become proficient in them. It is the same for a good driver who practices and develops good habits well in advance of needing those to save her life on a dangerous stretch of freeway, when an idiot does something scary in front of her.

I had a classmate in high school I refer to here as Azmina—you know why. She got top marks in almost all her courses and was generally considered a *braniac*, by me as well. Curiously, Azmina hit brick walls in one course, which baffled most of us at the time. Physics stumped her, the study of which often requires processing. The typical question on a physics exam is remarkably short, as is the answer. What gets you from question to answer is processing. Your work in that processing is often required to be included in an exam package to show how you got the answer. *Show your work* was the phrase my physics teacher frequently used. Marks were given for that work if some of it was right, even if the eventual answer was wrong. As it turned out, Azmina has an almost photographic memory, which served her well in many classes and not at all in at least one. Evidently, she had bucket loads of static knowledge but very little fluid knowledge, at least then.

In my day job as a college instructor, I appreciate the importance of training and education. Perhaps because of that, I also know of a few pitfalls that befall some people as they become trained or educated. These pitfalls don't make T & E bad things but they can make them *feel* like bad things. For that reason, it is in any learner's best interests to know and understand those pitfalls in advance, in part to lessen or neutralize their negative effects. Inasmuch as readers can be considered learners in a sense, I believe you should know about these pitfalls too.

As with so many aspects of what I've told you, I learned this from someone else, immediately thereafter recognizing many instances when I saw those pitfalls play out, and instances when I *felt* them play out. In his book *The Skillful Teacher,* Stephen Brookfield described several pitfalls in his chapter *Understanding and Responding to the Emotions of Learning.* While they don't all necessarily apply to people merely reading a book here and there, some of them can. I don't go into details here, which may not apply to you anyway. I merely identify them so you can recognize and address them if they arise for you or someone you know.

Brookfield identified *cultural suicide* as "the process whereby students are punished by their families, peers, and communities for what appears to be an act of betrayal"; that is, to be seen to change as a result of participating in learning. "This risk forces itself onto the consciousness of students of color in high school, as taking education seriously is condemned as 'acting White' (Bergin and Corks, 2002)." As Brookfield later pointed out, such issues can also face students who are the first of their family to go to college and it can affect many adult learners, in each case regardless of racial identities. "Cultural suicide is something that also affects working class students who 'often become alienated from their families in direct proportion to their procurement of new ideas and attitudes'".

I have seen that directly proportionate response occur within more affluent families, some that are 'White' too. One of my two best friends faced such a backlash from his father, who grew up in Hitler's Germany and couldn't fathom my friend's references to the Holocaust, which his father believed was blown out of all proportions. My friend's father saw friends and comrades die for that regime, so one could argue he was emotionally invested in the Holocaust being untrue. His teenaged son would say,

"Aw, c'mon, Papa, no more of that crap" when Papa played down ugly parts of that country's fairly recent history. Ugly or inconvenient truths can become an obstacle in many families, and new learning can contribute to those truths.

Brookfield described another pitfall as *lost innocence.*

> Students often come to campus with high hopes. They think that college will turn their lives around, that now they are going to get 'truth', and that finally they'll understand how the world really works and who they really are.

As Brookfield went on to explain, "When the penny drops and students realize their teachers mean what they say about there being no easy answers, universally correct views, or equivocally right ways to think, they panic."

In providing readers the full scoop, I may have prompted some to question some assumptions they hold, which can be a little unnerving. Assumptions can make things appear easy, comfortable, and safe. Even negative assumptions, such as a girl assuming she has no chance of success other than getting married and pregnant as soon as humanly possible, can be cognitively comforting since they relieve us of the perceived responsibility for making our own choices. In addition, many assumptions held by people serve the best interests of *other* people, such as young men who want young women to *know their place* and occupy that as soon as possible. While lost innocence can initially be unnerving, I liken it to in-line skating. At first glance, it would seem rather silly to be attached to that ground by only a single row of wheels instead of standing with two feet planted flatly on the ground. Standing on a row of wheels offers a swift fall with one wrong twitch. Over time, though, a novice can not only learn to balance and move with confidence but comfortably move at speeds far faster that anyone in normal footwear can. In the same way, lost innocence can turn into curiosity and then confidence in unknown lessons ahead. "I don't know what I'll find when I move forward," some successful learners think, "but it will be *something*, and probably better because it will be closer to the truth. It will be *real*."

The last of the pitfalls Brookfield identified was *roadrunning*, which isn't easily explained in a brief fashion. In his down to earth approach, Brookfield referred to the hapless coyote in the well-known *Roadrunner* cartoon. He wrote of how the coyote tried to catch the beep beeping little speedster time and again, often getting close and then falling off a cliff or being blown up or being crushed under the weight of an anvil, only to be whole and just as determined in the very next sequence.

In people who learn, this uneven rhythm plays itself out many times over. "Oh, I get this," you think one day, "this is actually quite simple". The very next day you might emotionally fall on your face, "God, I'll never understand that. It's beyond me, beyond my capabilities." New intellectual challenges can feel that way. Doing ten push ups is beyond the physical capabilities of someone who can only do five. However, those who work at five push ups every second day can then do six, then eight, and then, you get it. Similarly, what you do not understand right now is not usually beyond your abilities. It may only beyond your abilities *today*. With work and challenge, abilities adapt by increasing. That doesn't mean you won't feel like that hapless coyote from time to time. Still, understanding that we adapt and improve to meet the demands placed on us, whether by us or someone else, physically *and* mentally, will help dissolve the emotions that come with hitting those temporary walls of our seeming inability.

When looked at with reason and without excess emotion, none of these pitfalls are fatal despite the ominous terms used to describe them. Like BS itself, they are more easily navigated around when you know how to recognize them.

The modern automotive industry provides potentially fantastic products that enhance several people's lives at work, school, home and elsewhere. Cars can also be death traps. It all depends on how they are used. As well, education provides potentially wonderful opportunities for people to enhance their enjoyment and success whether at home, at work, or elsewhere in society. The habits with which we use our training and education, or our cars, determine the outcomes of those uses.

Habits that yield constructive, positive, helpful, and otherwise good outcomes are often the result of constructive training, provided in a formal setting by mentors, or by you *for* you. I was very fortunate to have Tim Zayack as a boss for a few years. He is very bright, became well educated in his middle years, is married to a wonderful woman with two PhDs, and he's as gruff as you would expect of a steel worker's son from Sudbury, Ontario (think Pittsburg if you're American or Sheffield if you're English). He imparted great knowledge and built good habits in his workers, with gentle intellect or a verbal sledge hammer, whichever needs dictated. Little of that training impacted directly on our work but that hardly mattered to Tim. For instance, Tim hated to hear oral fillers such as *um* and *uh*. I cannot quote him because I have committed to no profanity within these pages, but he used to rail against me so often when I used an oral fillers that I developed the habit of stopping to think before using them, as did many other people around Tim. If he wasn't swearing when he delivered this particular bit of training, it might have come out like this: *When you don't know what word to use, stop and think until you come up with the word. Don't throw out something useless that isn't a word at all.*

In doing what he did and how he did it, Tim demonstrated a few important lessons about training. Since we were city workers dealing with troubled people, our work environment was not intentionally educational or meant for training. Be that as it may, both happened regularly because bosses like Tim made sure we collectively learned from everything that went right and everything that went wrong. Teaching happened because Tim recognized two important things:

- Something or someone can often be improved in some way.
- Opportunities for improvement often require learning, and these same opportunities provide great opportunities for teaching.

Like many groups, professional educators have their own shop talk. What I describe above with the second bullet point is often referred to in educators' circles as *teaching moments*. Amateur educators rarely use such lingo or consciously think about seizing on those. They simply take opportunities, day in and day out, to teach people by explaining, by leading with examples, by correcting, by praising, and by discussing. You might wonder who these amateur educators are. I refer to parents, bosses, coaches, music producers, plumbers, dog owners, and plenty of others.

When a child drops food on the couch, Mom or Dad is less than pleased and wants it cleaned up, but parents also want junior to not eat in the living room, or to do so more carefully. So they take steps to make that happen. In doing so, they realize Junior will probably make the same mistake again, like he did before. Still, they seize this teaching moment because they know that not doing so will all but guarantee that Junior will keep making the same mistake, and make it more often.

Because teaching moments occur regularly and without warning, a lot of teaching and a lot of learning can take place with little to no preparation, and with no additional effort on anyone's part. Tossing a ball with your kid, walking the dog, eating dinner with the family, shooting the breeze with the teens you coach in hockey or teach in music. All of these provide countless opportunities for teaching moments, each time the kid or dog or under study does something incorrectly (requiring correction) or correctly (deserving praise). Every compliment reinforces skills or good habits, or both.

Training to develop solid BS busting skills can be self driven. If you don't already, soak up information from reading, television, life experiences, and work experiences. Then process that. Form opinions. Express and defend them. Most important, be willing to change those opinions if or when you get new information that weakens your own positions.

Even the most intractable political parties change over years as circumstances outside of them and people within them change, and as time passes. In the mid nineteenth century in the United States, the upstart Republican Party helped Abraham Lincoln become President. During the ensuing American Civil War, Lincoln and his Republicans aggressively prosecuted that war, the end of which ended lawful slavery in the U.S. Throughout that war, the Democrats wanted peace at any price even if it meant continuation of slavery in the southern states. Decades later on the eve of the Second World War, the Republicans were staunchly *against* the U.S. entering any foreign war. The ruling Democrats figured America's involvement was inevitable and best prepared for as soon as possible. Only after Imperial Japan attacked the American naval base at Pearl Harbour (Hawaii), did the U.S. join that war. When the Vietnam War came along, it was again a Democratic president who first sent men overseas. More recently, the

Republicans are seen as the more hawk like folks in the U.S. and less responsive to the needs of visible minority groups. What comes around goes around and around and around, in America and elsewhere. Such is the nature of thought and argument in the face of ever changing circumstances.

The nature of thought, arguments, and the decisions which flow from both, is of particular interest to a growing number of companies and people. For example, Aaron Barth's Dialectic Strategies (dialecticstrategies. com) provides group training to companies interested in improving how to consciously think, explain their thinking, and make decisions. Remarkably few corporations invest in training for academic or leisurely purposes; the diverse and considerable number of Barth's clients speaks volumes about the effectiveness and value of thinking about thinking, of thinking consciously, clearly, and effectively. As a PhD and associate professor of philosophy, he's no academic slouch either. Through learning how to think about their thinking, these companies are evolving into stronger, progressive, highly adaptable entities.

Of course, individual people can philosophically and intellectually evolve as well. Also, that individual evolution can be positive or negative or both. For example, U.S. President Barack Obama previously supported gay rights but not gay marriage, yet his opinion changed over several years to where he now supports it. Opinion polls indicate the same shift in opinion has occurred in many Americans over the same approximate time period. Sometimes circumstances change, sometimes people change or at least significant numbers of them do.

Racism and other forms of prejudice are not genetically inherited by people. They are learned, as are open-mindedness, tolerance, and understanding. Ironically, some people who seek more equitable treatment for one group or another can inadvertently promote less equitable treatment of other groups. Prejudice is, after all, prejudging regardless of what direction the subsequent erroneous beliefs point.

Is a tattoo on the small of a women's back an example of edgy art or a *tramp stamp*? Is a kid wearing his pants so low the crotch of his pants hangs around his knees a cool fashion statement, emulation of urban gangs, or does this kid simply not know how to put pants on? What is more known by the general population, the whereabouts of Paris, France or Paris Hilton? For most folks, questions like these are fairly harmless.

There are other questions, though. Is global warming a reality or merely the war cry of tree huggers? Are cultural differences programmed into everyone's genes or are they a product of customs and culture, which change over time as groups adapt? Is there a point to participating in elections, and if so, how can you make things more to your liking? These questions and thousands of others lurk out there for millions of people to consider, to challenge, and to try answering.

Another step follows discussion and thought: action. I'm not telling anyone what to think, much less what to do. As colleague, friend, and community leader Steve Hicks says, "Make a difference; make it happen". What *it* is will depend on what matters to you.

Many people view education and to some extent training as an academic exercise, of tangible use to very few. That brings me to answering a question posed in the first paragraph of this chapter, what training and education has to do with BS.

Education and its close relative training are of little use when wasted, yet they can be so much more when put to constructive use. Educated, engaged people can disagree and often do. As long as various people with various beliefs do *something*, make *something constructive* happen, progress will be made on thousands of fronts. Since

BS stems from a lack of intellectual effort as much as anything, engaged thoughts followed by engaged actions lessens poop's influence, if not also its impact.

If you already have an education, use it, if you don't use it already. If you don't have an education, get one by whatever constructive means you can. As for training, find a mentor or be your own. Repetition is aggravating for some people yet vital for many people to develop constructive habits. Although repetition is usually considered poor form in writing, I use it frequently in one form or another in these pages to help some readers train themselves, and because I'm a repetitive bastard. How's *that* for no BS?

Let's end with the most important questions of all:

What matters to *you*, whoever you are? What do *you* think about it? Based on what? Most importantly, what will you *do* about it? And, in doing whatever you do, will you help spread malignant BS piles or join the movement against it?

The first step in this movement is to think consciously. As an earlier mentioned example, Aaron Barth teaches corporate personnel the the art and science of "thinking about thinking" with his Dialectic Strategies. Barth's blogs are terrific and informative too, and can be found at dialecticstrategies.com. There is no end to the benefits of conscious, logical thought, including effective group and corporate decisions.

I hope you choose to fight malignant BS piles. I hope you make it a habit, if it isn't already your habit, to think consciously and reasonably, to repel malignant BS, and to encourage others to do all three too. I would be less than honest if I didn't say that will help me, but it will immeasurably help you too. Honest. No BS.

APPENDIX A

OTHER PEOPLE'S TAKE ON BS

For better or for worse, I regularly point out extra bits of information to readers and listeners. The latter group are usually students who may not be as much captivated as captive. Among my regular points is this: I didn't invent anything I discuss or teach or write about. I merely tried to approach topics differently. Of course, that's what many writers do. What I discussed and delved into with this book, and that I hope some readers will discuss and delve into in their lives, has been addressed in various ways by other people. It appears, then, that BS matters to at least some others too. Therefore, I alert you to some of those other people, or their work, so you can check them out if you choose.

I previously mentioned Professor Harry Frankfurt's essay, *On (BS)*, a short, inspiring work I highly recommend. In a sense, this book is my attempt to expand on his clear definitions of BS. *On (BS)* is available on its own and as part of *The Importance of What We Care About,* both from Cambridge Press.

Your Call Is Very Important To Us: The Truth About (BS), by Laura Penney, is another book I previously mentioned, mainly regarding the importance of language skills in reducing BS susceptibility. Penney's book examined aspects of everyday BS in the media, advertising, and other arenas of human contact. I read her book many years ago while writing an earlier work. That is when I recognised the correlation between language skills and avoiding BS, as well as the correlation between BS and varied bad outcomes in life. Although Penney's book didn't seem to address the fundamental aspects of BS that make it so ubiquitous in our lives, that appears not to have been her objective. I greatly enjoyed reading her book, which provided several important conceptual connections for which I am grateful. Penney's book was published by McLelland & Stewart.

Without Penney's book hitting a mark I increasingly thought about, I sought out another book to do that. I came up empty, which may speak to the lack of such a previous work or poor researching by me. Hence, I began my own written foray into BS. As the length and tone of this book may suggest, this book wasn't a horrible labour for me. I enjoyed it, learned a few things, and had a few laughs along the way. I hope I've been able to help you learn a bit and have a few laughs too. Although I didn't find anyone or anything providing what I refer to as the *full scoop* on this topic, I found other sources addressing one aspect of BS or another.

At the tail end of my edits of this book, I picked up *I Call (BS): Debunking the Most Commonly Repeated Myths,* by Jamie Frater, founder of listverse.com. Published by Ulysses Press, it was a light, easy to pick up read with a simple format: a short, commonly-repeated myth was identified, followed by a concise and often-humorous debunking of said myth. That raises a few minor but relevant points on this topic.

First, most myths qualify as BS. Jamie Frater obviously believed that or he wouldn't have put myth and (BS) in the same title/subtitle. A well-known television show directly addressed myths, but I address that shortly.

Second, did I mention Frater's debunking was short? Truth often involves details that are difficult to convey without words, numeric data, or both. Quite often, entertainment can be achieved with far fewer details. That's why, for instance, I imagine CSI is less fun to watch if you're a police officer with forensic experience. *I Call (BS)* would perhaps be less entertaining if it was bogged down in details. Frater managed most of his debunking within a page or so, with lots of entertainment along the way.

Third, some myths are so stinky that very little information is needed to debunk them. In those cases, the information can be well known and simply not remembered by many until someone reminds them, after which that *oh yeah* moment occurs, a feeling we all get once in a while. Frater did a great job on a diverse range of myths. In a small minority of cases, those myths may not have been as well debunked. Here's one example from *I Call (BS)*:

> MYTH: The Middle Ages were splattered with the blood of those who died of the death penalty.
>
> (BS)! The Middle Ages gave birth to the jury system, and trials were in fact very fair. The death penalty was considered to be extremely severe and was used only in the worst crimes like murder, treason and arson. It was not until the Middle Ages drew to a close that rulers such as Elizabeth I began to use the death penalty as a means to get rid of their nation's religious opponents . . .

That debunking and what followed *could* be true; however, a variety of academic and historical sources suggest otherwise. For starters, the last book I read before Frater's was Allen C. Hutchison's *Is Eating People Wrong? Great Legal Cases and How They Shaped the World.* Hutchison is an oft-published law professor at Osgoode Hall (York University in Toronto). His book explained eight famous cases that influenced and still shape fundamental legal principles in several nations, an area referred to within those circles as *the common law.* The cases were from the United Kingdom, the United States, Canada, and Australia, the earliest one dating back to the early 19th century. Hutchison made clear from the outset that the law and application of it are both works in progress, as are the societies that shape the law, apply it, or turn to it in times of dispute. He also made no bones about how little the outcomes sometimes had to do with fairness.

Exhibit 1: In the *Hadley v. Baxendale* decision of 1854 in England, two of the four appeals judges had close connections to Joseph Baxendale, respondent and managing director of Pickford and Company. A brother of one judge was the immediate predecessor to Baxendale as Pickford's managing director, and another was previously Pickford's standing counsel for many years. Either instance would have been a clear conflict of interest and rarely accepted today, let alone two such instances on the same case. That doesn't mean their judgement was wrong. It is hailed as a balanced decision and studied by law students in several countries today. Still, one could easily argue that the matter was not decided fairly, especially since the decision favoured Baxendale and Pickford's.

As for juries, history is filled with instances of unfair verdicts. In parts of the United States where former jurors are allowed to speak with the press after trials, some jurors even take issue with their *own* verdicts. That often happens after they find out something that was judicially withheld and would have influenced their decision. Cultural, racial, religious, and gender biases have also plagued trials in many parts of the world for centuries.

As for folks before Elizabeth I not being murderous, consider that Elizabeth's father was Henry VIII, who had a number of people put to death, including some former wives, one being Elizabeth's mother, Anne Bolyn. Elizabeth's sister was Queen Mary, known better as *Bloody Mary* and not because she was a bartender. She was a fierce Catholic related to, and also married into, the Spanish royal family. Mary reportedly had many Protestants put to death in England. In fairness, she may have been pressured by her husband, whose empire then included the Vatican. The preferred method of dispatching these so called heathens was burning at the stake, so I suppose an argument can be made that the Middle Ages were not so much bloody as charred, but you get the idea. Some reports have Mary pardoning as many as 400 people, both so called heretics and rebels trying to overthrow her. Still, an estimated 275 to 300 people were executed in her name, let alone the numbers killed in the name of other monarchs and powerful folks. Interesting tidbits are available about a host of other monarchs from the Middle Ages. I suggest you check out *Vlad the Impaler* to start with, who may have had thousands killed. From his nickname, you can probably guess how. Also, if you have seen the movie *Braveheart*, consider that the gruesome punishment for treason depicted in the film, hanging and disembowelling before beheading and dismemberment, was toned down for film from the actual punishment for treason followed by England for many centuries. Last but not least, treason reportedly underwent liberal interpretations by many rulers throughout history.

None of those details detract from the entertainment aspect of *I Call (BS)*. My details on one myth alone run much longer than any of Frater's debunkings, and his book might have been the poorer for such detail. From what I can tell, the vast majority of his debunking was accurate, and helpful to anyone paying even a little attention. Whatever may be incorrect was mistaken despite efforts not to be. Hence, his work was not BS.

This book is *not* intended to be the last word on misinformation or a detailed academic examination of it. Neither is Frater's, which I still recommend. It is plenty entertaining and informative. Light, entertaining reading is still reading. Learning a *little* something here and there is still learning. My reason for pointing out a potential shortfall in his book isn't to slam Jamie Frater, merely to illustrate that with many topics, you can drill down deeper, give something a harder or more sceptical look. You can also have fun with just a surface look at this or that. Sometimes short *is* sweet provided other sustenance is taken in from time to time.

The popular television show I referred to earlier is aptly titled *Mythbusters,* widely available on the Discovery Channel. It took a scientific approach to whatever they tackled. Their science didn't usually involve test tubes or laboratories but, without exception, it involved reasoning and putting theories to the test. In a nutshell, that is what is sometimes referred to as the *scientific method.* In some instances, the myths were confirmed, other times busted— hence the show's name—and sometimes neither confirmed nor busted; rather they were listed as plausible or possible. Their methods made the show fun to watch and probably more fun to perform. Beneath the booms, bangs, laughs, and self-deprecating humour, the show's cast regularly demonstrated the scientific method of examination and professional scepticism, often concerning every day issues and myths. Some of the information was potentially life-saving too.

There were a few lesser known shows that differed considerably from *Mythbusters* while still addressing BS head on. Chief among those from my point of view was

Penn & Teller: (BS)!. It was broadcast by ShowTime and many episodes or parts thereof are available on YouTube. You may recognize the names Penn and Teller for their wild acts that are equal part illusion, comedy, and thought provocation. Penn Gilette is a mountain of a man with a voice and personality to match. Teller, who legally has no first name, is his polar opposite in many ways. Teller is physically small, he never speaks publicly, and his manner is as unassuming as you can imagine. They make a terrific team and I suspect Teller is every bit as much the brains of the outfit as his big working partner.

Their BS-related shows were short and often hilarious. Penn was none too shy with profanity in these shows, not just the actual term for BS but other words I'm none too shy with using either (outside of my writing this). The show concerned BS of such a high level as to be wildly profane. Sometimes a little profanity is needed to wake some people up. *Penn & Teller: (BS)!* mocked varied myths, issues, and beliefs. In their seventh season alone, their list included cheerleaders, martial arts, easy money, and paranoia over child vaccinations. Their method of examination/mockery was about as subtle as a proctologist might be while wearing boxing gloves. I don't agree with every target or opinion they had but I agree with most of them. Even when I didn't agree, I found their shows hilarious, and educational. It was described as debunking (BS) through critical thinking and reason. Hmm, that sounds a bit famili . . . never mind. As the show's web site stated (in part), "As our increasingly anti-intellectual, anti-science culture moves on each day to new crackpot subject matters, Penn & Teller are there to aggressively shoot down whack jobs and fuzzy thinkers, no matter where they originate."

Last but certainly not least in the quest for less BS was Carl Sagan's *The Demon Haunted World: Science as a Candle in the Dark,* published shortly after the author's death in 1996. Sagan was an astrophysicist, cosmologist, professor of astronomy, the writer and host of the television series *Cosmos: A Personal Voyage,* and the author of over 20 books. *The Demon Haunted World* concerned the scientific method, and it triumphed inquiry and skepticism, the hallmarks of science. In his opening chapter, Sagan wrote of being retrieved from an airport by a man who, knowing Sagan as a famous scientist, wanted to pick his brain on a number of topics. Sagan was happy to oblige yet what the man asked about were myths of varied proportions ranging from frozen extraterrestrials to channelling with dead people to astrology and so on. Sagan reluctantly shattered each of the man's beliefs, which appeared to be based on highly questionable sources,

> Mr 'Buckley'—well-spoken, intelligent, curious—had heard virtually nothing of modern science. He had a natural appetite for the wonders of the Universe. He wanted to know about science. It's just that all the science had gotten filtered out before it reached him. Our cultural motifs, our educational system, our communications media had failed this man. What society permitted to trickle through was mainly pretence and confusion. It had never taught him how to distinguish real science from the cheap imitation. He knew nothing about how science works.

Sagan's book went on to explain how science works. Accordingly, one of his book's chapters was entitled *The Fine Art of Baloney Detection.* Of course, *baloney,* like balderdash and similar terms, is virtually synonymous with BS. Sagan's chapter took aim at the same ubiquitous nonsense that others and I did. Citing a variety of dubious ideas and beliefs, from the healing powers of a violet flame to the baseless claims of many analgesic marketers (against competitors who market the same ingredients) to a wide variety of clairvoyants, he wrote, "These are all cases of proved or presumptive baloney. A deception arises, sometimes innocently but collaboratively, sometimes with cynical premeditation. Usually the victim is caught up in a powerful emotion—wonder, fear, greed, grief."

Initially ignorant of his work, I still arrived at the same conclusions, and wrote about them in familiar terms. This isn't to compare my intellect with Sagan's; there is no comparison. It is merely to suggest that when well-known academics and inquiring lay people wind up with similar results despite varied methodologies, the probability of their beliefs being true is often considerable. Similarly, Sagan recognized the dangers in a lack of criticality being the norm.

> Credulous acceptance of baloney can cost you money . . . But it can be much more dangerous than that, and when governments and societies lose the capacity for critical thinking, the results can be catastrophic, however sympathetic we may be to those who have bought the baloney.

Within these pages, I tried to put a humorous take on the importance of reasoning, in part to bring more everyday people into that fold. As Sagan made clear, a collective lack of that capacity can be catastrophic. To combat this threat, he suggested a *tool kit* filled for sceptical thinking. Many of those tools are the same common fallacies I described in the Reasoning chapter, yet he included others such as fact confirmation, thinking up multiple hypotheses, not getting too committed to one theory because it's yours, and consistency of approach. For that reason and how enjoyable Sagan's writing is, I strongly recommend *The Demon Haunted World*.

Although none of the books or shows defined BS or myth, they each demonstrated a solid grasp of what it is. This leads to my last point concerning other people's work on this topic. It concerns meanings, discussed earlier in the Language and Reasoning chapters. The first task in verbal expression is choosing words to explain what you think or feel. You can make up your own words, but who will understand them? You need words that are understood by other people. If you read a book written fifty or a hundred years ago, you will see many differences in the use of words, and many words that aren't used today. William Shakespeare's work from over four centuries ago used structure and words far different from today's language. Many words evolve to include or discard certain meanings.

An excellent tool for improving verbal skills is a dictionary, often the best source of choosing effective words, yet many people misunderstand dictionaries' role in language. Dictionaries do not dictate what words people should use for various thoughts; just the opposite. For instance, you could create the word *blixing* to describe the act of removing fungus from under toenails. If no one else uses that word, it will die with you. If other people start using it the same way, and the word catches on with more and more people, it could eventually wind up in common English and then in dictionaries. Thus, a dictionary merely defines what most people mean when they use this word or that.

BS is what it is defined as, not because some dictionaries may say so right now, because Harry Frankfurt said so, or because any of the folks I referred above implied so. What matters is that a number of seemingly smart people appeared to understand exactly what they were talking about when they discussed, attacked, or satirized BS.

In the Preface of this book, I made it clear that many every-day people do not understand what BS truly is. True though that may be, a number of people obviously do. Each of those people is mentally engaged, not just with attacking BS but with a whole range of subjects and matters. Each is successful in one way or another. Each is aware of their surroundings and is navigating those very well, thank you very much. The thing is, so are you, now if not also before. Imagine that.

APPENDIX B

INDICATORS AND REVELATIONS

Armed with the BS busting skills you hopefully have now, or that you can develop with practice, I invite you to compile your own list below. If you feel like sharing them, please send me a copy of your list to duncanbooks.com. If you take issue with any indicators from my list, please feel equally welcomed to share that. I've still got plenty to learn.

Indicator/Revelation: _____

Details of indicator/revelation: _____

_____

_____

_____

_____

Indicator/Revelation: _____

Details of indicator/revelation: _____

_____

_____

_____

_____

Indicator/Revelation: _____

Details of indicator/revelation: _____

_____

_____

_____

_____

Indicator/Revelation: _____

Details of indicator/revelation: _____

_____

_____

_____

_____

Indicator/Revelation: _____

Details of indicator/revelation: _____

_____

_____

_____

_____

Indicator/Revelation: _____

Details of indicator/revelation: _____

_____

_____

_____

_____

Indicator/Revelation: _____

Details of indicator/revelation: _____

_____

_____

_____

_____

Indicator/Revelation: _____

Details of indicator/revelation: _____

_____

_____

_____

_____

Indicator/Revelation: _____

Details of indicator/revelation: _____

_____

_____

_____

_____

APPENDIX C

WHAT YOU CARE ABOUT

You don't know me and may not even care to know me but you have likely attained a sense of what I am about, at least in some ways. More to the point, you likely have a sense of at least some of the things I care about, certainly not all of them but at least a few. Naturally, what I care about shouldn't matter to you nearly as much as what *you* care about. What may be more surprising to you is that, at least for now, I'm also more interested in what you care about. No BS.

I already know what *I* care about. What I don't have a clue about is what readers of this book think about or care about, what they might want to change or see changed by someone else, that sort of thing. I crave new information and topics, and new ways of looking at old information and topics. Nothing of what *I* think or care about is new to *me*.

Within the preceding pages I addressed several aspects of life that bug me, as well as why they bug me. With that out of my system, I'm much more interested in finding out what bugs or thrills or engages other people including you, whoever the heck you are. That can provide me new stuff to ponder and perhaps write about or engage in myself.

For that reason, I ask you to take some time to consider what you care about and then commit that to paper or an electronic alternative. I'm just as interested in *why* you care about whatever you do, what you would like to see done about it, what *you* would like to do about it, and/or what you have already done.

You may not consciously care about much at all right now. If so, fair enough. Thoughtful engagement takes time and mental energy, neither of which are in an endless supply for any of us. Still, the more you find the time and energy, or make them, the more effortless it will become to care about things. On the other side of the coin, you may care about dozens of topics, in which case writing them down from time to time can be helpful, if only to avert a feeling of being overwhelmed by a staggering list of issues.

Of course, you don't *have* to share anything with me, or anyone for that matter. We both know I have no way of making that happen anyway. Nevertheless, the first person you may actually be revealing things to is yourself. That's who really matters most and matters first when it comes to your thoughts. The outside world comes later, if at all.

On that note, let me share a quick tip with you from author Stephen King that may help you with your thoughts and recording those. For the purposes of this tip, I don't think it matters if you will write for publication and profit or a confidential journal. In his book *On Writing*, King asked readers to consider what the most valuable and necessary tool is for one who writes. I've asked several people that question (only because of King asking me and his other readers), so I know the answers often vary from a good personal computer to a good dictionary or a comfy chair. The answer is *a door*. That allows us all time and space to throw onto paper (or the electronic equivalent) what's in our heads without worrying about other people peeking in on early versions of our thoughts or words, which we often rethink or restate over and over again before we are ready to share those. I believe such time and space is not only helpful but necessary. If you later share your cares or words with someone else, that will be a big step for you, and quite possibly a great experience for those you share with. If you also share them with me, I will be grateful. If you learn a thing or three about yourself in the process, that will be a bonus. Suggesting this exercise was just a thought, but just about anything starts that way, doesn't it?

I can be reached at duncanbooks.com.

ACKNOWLEDGEMENTS

Almost no undertaking occurs in a vacuum, and this book was no different. In addition to the various writers, performers, and lesser-known people I referred to in preceding pages, I am indebted to several people for direct assistance.

My thanks go to Robin Murray and Markus Schwegler for early feedback, Kerry Watkins for the push of an experienced writer late in my efforts, Jon Ling for endless patience while working with me on my day job, Stuart Blower for honest feedback and proof reading, and Laima Gravelson for further proof reading late in the game.

I shudder to think how this book would have been without that help. Any errors or omissions are all mine.

ABOUT THE AUTHOR

Peter Duncan was born in Edmonton, Alberta and raised throughout Western Canada, predominantly in Vancouver, BC. He lives in Toronto.

For over two decades Duncan has worked in the public safety field as well as voluntarily with at-risk youth and on issues involving them.

Duncan currently teaches at a Toronto area college.